Planning and Building Your Home Workshop

by David X. Manners

POPULAR SCIENCE BOOKS

HARPER & ROW, PUBLISHERS

NEW YORK, SAN FRANCISCO, HAGERSTOWN, LONDON

Manufactured in the United States of America

Cover photo courtesy of David Warren and Hedrich-Blessing

Contents

This book is dedicated . . .

Not to the craftsmen of yesterday and the
old ways of doing things, but to Paul, Jon,
Mike and Tim and all the craftsmen of tomorrow
who will be doing things better than their fathers
and grandfathers.

1

Ten Places
to Put a Workshop

Every homeowner needs a workshop to keep his house in good shape. Even if a shop did not pay for itself in the money you save doing your own repairs, it would be worthwhile for the pleasure it offers. But usually a shop does help you save money. When repairs must be made you are at no one's mercy. You may mangle a few jobs at first, but you will be learning, developing your skills. Also, you will be better prepared to oversee those jobs you assign to others, and a better judge of workmanship and cost. In this age of technology a man is handicapped if he's baffled by a malfunctioning dishwasher, a balky oil burner, or the intricacies of a printed circuit.

There are at least ten good places you can put a shop. There are countless ways to create space where there seems to be none. In planning where to put a shop, think of the kinds of jobs you want to do in it.

The maintenance of a house involves carpentry, plumbing, electrical work, metalwork, painting and paperhanging, masonry, landscaping and gardening, roofing, and repairing and refinishing furniture. A place may be needed for hi-fi, ham

An orderly, attractive shop makes working a pleasure. Such a shop could be built in a garage, basement, or spare room. Inexpensive pine boards and decorative iron hardware lend a pleasant appearance.

radio, or electronics, working with plastics, leather, old clocks, or antique toys. Other activities may include gunmaking, modelmaking, welding, repairing gasoline engines, automobiles, and boats. A shop may be a creative center for the entire family, with workbenches for the children, girls as well as boys.

BASEMENT SHOPS.   More shops are in the basement than anywhere else. It has major advantages as well as some drawbacks. On the plus side, it is warm in winter, cool in summer. It is quiet, and you can mess it up. It may also be dark, dingy, cobwebbed, damp, or subject to periodic flooding. A damp basement creates rust problems. A flooded basement can be a disaster. But these are difficulties that can be overcome.

New foam boards can be used to insulate basement walls and check dampness. Applying epoxy waterproofing to walls from the inside, grading slopes away from the basement walls on the ontside, and repairing leaking gutters and downspouts may be all that is required to prevent flooding. A good sump pump is added insurance. A false ceiling can hide plumbing, wiring, and ductwork. Ceiling panels may be removed for access. A load-bearing cabinet can support a weak or sagging floor overhead.

A basement shop benefits from sufficient light and air. If basement windows are below grade, recessed in a well, this areaway can sometimes be extended and additional windows installed. On walls paralleling floor joists, stock 18"-by-32" windows can be set in a continuous ribbon, using 2"-by-8" or 2"-by-10" verticals to support the first-floor plates. You can even install windows in walls which support floor joists by inserting supports, such as 3" pipe, every few feet, If your basement does not have good access to the outdoors, provide one. Prefab stairway assemblies and low-cost metal doors for the entrance make the job easier.

Some basements are difficult to remodel because they were

A full basement is divided with a two-way workbench in the shop of architect Paul R. MacAlister. Openness of design improves lighting and aids ventilation.

4

White walls and drawer fronts lend a light, cheerful accent to this basement shop. Heating system in the basement keeps it warm and dry.

Replacing old, bulky heating plant with a compact modern system frees basement space for a shop. This one is in a former coal bin.

built improperly. If you are building or buying a house here's what to watch for in a basement:

- If basement walls are of concrete block, they should be at least twelve blocks high. The usual basement is built only eleven blocks high and this produces a ceiling just over 7′ high, too low for a good shop. The added cost is relatively small.

- Pipes and electrical cables should run between the joists instead of below them. Keep warm-air ducts at the perimeter of the basement.

- Be sure the basement is waterproofed correctly. The exterior block walls should receive a coating of cement plaster. A heavy coating of asphalt waterproofing compound should go over this. The first two courses of block should be solid, and if there is any question at all about drainage, install a line of drain tile around the wall's footings, to lead off the water.

GARAGE SHOPS.   Getting a shop in a single-car garage is difficult. If you have 3′ at one end it can be managed: A 2′ bench leaves 1′ clearance for working. If you have 3′ to spare on one side, you can install a compact shop along this wall. Tools and sawhorses can be moved to the main area for large projects. If a garage isn't wide enough to accommodate a shop, you can add a bay to increase its width.

Switching to a compact car can free space in the garage for a shop. Storage is an important part of any shop. Space above the hood of a car is ordinarily wasted. Use it. In building locker space over the hood, allow a 6″ clearance. Storage lockers on one or both sides of the car can help support the crossing structure. Use sliding panels on the lockers, and you won't have to worry about swing space. Make the panels of ¼″ plywood or hardboard. Sliding track for the panels is available at your lumberyard.

Create loft storage under a pitched roof. Hang storage from the rafters. It's a good place for ladders. Get the most out of space by categorizing it: lawn and garden tools in one place, camping equipment in another, and barbecuing gear in a third.

BEFORE. This garage was nothing but a wasted space for haphazard storage. Converting it into a workshop with organized storage is really a simple job.

AFTER. Storage and organization bring order out of chaos and put waste space to work. Walls and cabinetwork are of knotty Ponderosa pine. *Courtesy Western Wood Products.*

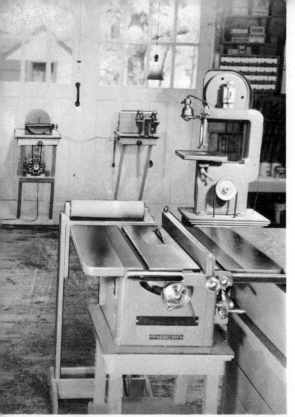

In this garage shop, sander and grinder are mounted on brackets attached to the doors to use space that would otherwise be wasted.

Table saw and band saw occupy center of the same shop, with workbench and storage cabinets along the far wall. Combination cabinet-work support stores accessories for table saw.

By adding a carport, a double garage becomes available for a shop. One of the garage doors was replaced by two windows, the other was left intact to facilitate moving materials and projects in and out.

Christmas decorations, luggage, and dead storage can go on the highest shelves. If the storage is closed off by doors, it can present a neat appearance.

A garage shop is ideal if you plan to work on your car. A drain pit is important in such a setup. A typical size is 32″ by 60″, with depth to accommodate your height. Masonry blocks are an easy-to-use material. At the bottom of the pit, a 2′-by-2′-by-2′ hole filled with gravel can provide drainage. The pit should be covered with a door when not in use.

If you need more light in your garage, but don't want to expose the interior to outside view, use textured glass. Prefab window units come in many sizes, and installation requires only the preparation of an opening. In a frame garage, simply install panes of glass between the studs, using molding strips. If desired, glass can be run all the way up to the gabled peaks. Again, use textured glass to block the view.

To get added light into the garage, place glass in some of the panels in a solid garage door. Cut out the panels, set in glass with quarter-round molding.

Prefab plastic skylight units are another way to bring light into the garage shop. Most skylights require no flashing or special framing. A ribbon of mastic is placed around the prepared opening, and the skylight is nailed through its flange directly to the roof.

An important advantage of the shop in a garage is that trucks can deliver materials directly to it.

An easy way to enlarge a garage is to extend one roof slope 8′. An 8′-by-16′ extension not only provides space for a workshop, but also for storing garden tools and outdoor equipment.

Here is how to figure how much space your garage can spare for shop or storage: Your car requires its full width, plus the width of one door fully opened. It also requires its full length plus 2′. The rest of the space is yours. If garage walls are open studs, insulate them and cover them with half-inch plasterboard before building cabinets.

You may find it advantageous to build a carport for your car and take over the garage for your shop. In some cases a car may not even demand shelter. A garage offers prime space for conversion into a shop. Drive around town and look for garage conversions. The best will be hardest to spot.

ATTIC SHOPS.   Attics are often hot in summer and short on headroom. It is difficult to transport materials and supplies to and from an attic, and the noise of a shop and its dust carry down into the rest of the house. But these are drawbacks that can be lived with, or in some cases overcome.

If the attic is hot, install a ventilating fan. It will not only reduce the attic temperature, but will cool off the rest of the house. Painting the roof white can also reduce attic temperature. Special paints are available for the purpose.

You can cut down on noise by mounting power tools on rubber mats. Indoor-outdoor carpeting can muffle noises through the floor.

If your garage has a steeply pitched roof, there may be

Well-insulated attic workshop has workbench in the center and near window, most power tools along the eaves (above). Deep storage cabinets are built into the other low-headroom side (right).

enough space under it for a shop. For a 12′ span, 2″-by-6″ joists on 16″ centers are usually adequate to support the floor. A quick floor can be made of sheathing-grade plywood. An inexpensive folding stairway can give access to the deck.

ENCLOSE A PORCH.   Many porches are seldom used. Often, only part of a porch is needed to provide adequate shop space and the rest left open for entry purposes. Enclosing a porch is neither as difficult nor as expensive as building a complete structure. Roof, floor, and one or perhaps two walls already exist. Filling in the rest is a cinch.

A porch may provide ample space for a shop. The floor, roof, and one wall already exist; only three walls must be added. This porch shop features a workbench built on top of a steel filing cabinet.

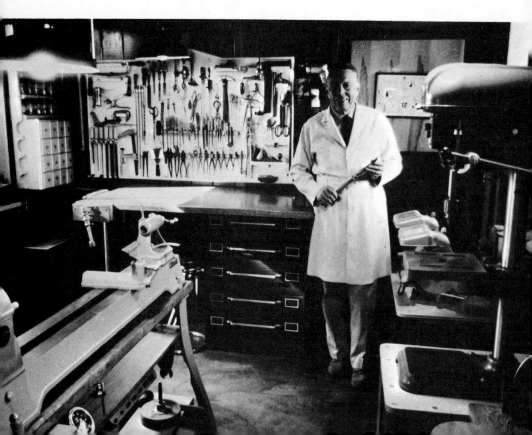

SPARE-ROOM SHOPS.   A bedroom, or any other spare room, can be taken over for a shop. The two big problems are noise and dust. Rooms are difficult to soundproof, which may limit your activities at some hours. They are also difficult to dustproof. A tight-fitting door may help, but how about the sawdust you track out on your shoes? And how will the dust that clings to the windowpanes look from outside the house?

Good light, heat, and ventilation are some of the happier assets of the spare-room shop. It often provides a more alluring aspect than having to descend into the basement or trek out to the garage.

Spare room in a city apartment was turned into a complete workshop with acoustical tile and wood paneling to soften noises. Shop is illuminated by overhead recessed fluorescent lights, even has a built-in sink for washing up.

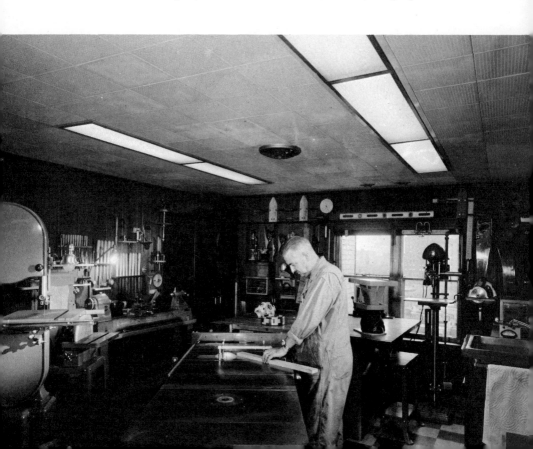

CLOSET SHOPS.   With a little ingenuity, an amazing amount of tool storage and work space can be fitted into a closet. Highly productive shops have been hung on the back of a closet door, with work tables that fold down to reveal an array of hand tools neatly stored on panel of perforated hardboard. It's not an ideal solution, but it's a beginning. There may be space under a stairway or at the end of a hall that can provide comparable accommodations.

OUTBUILDING SHOPS.   If a house is small, without a basement, and there is no room in the garage, a separate building may be the answer. In it you can work late at night or in the early-morning hours without disturbing anyone. A precut garage may be an inexpensive way to get such a shop. Or how about a trailer?

One man bought an inexpensive 10′-by-14′ chicken house and used this prefab package for his shop. The 2″-by-3″

In mild climates tools can be kept in a storage house and wheeled out on sun-shaded platform for use. A cramped garage shop can be similarly extended outdoors.

and 1″-by-4″ roosts made shelves and benches. An intercom links it to the house. Such a structure is ideal for boatbuilding and other large projects.

Existing barns and outbuildings may afford prime shop space. Insulation and heating may have to be provided, possibly a power line run out to it, but it is only a remodeling job. Most people would rather remodel than attempt to build from scratch. In some areas, codes may stop you from adding an additional structure on your property, but an existing structure doesn't pose any problem.

OUTDOOR SHOPS.   If you live in a mild climate, you can keep power tools and bench inside in storage spaces and roll them out when you want to work. A blacktop or concrete slab is a necessity for easy rolling and simple cleanup.

THE CABINET TRICK.   That fine piece of furniture you see in someone's apartment living room may not be what it appears to be. It may open up in several directions to reveal a complete workbench. Plans for a cabinet-workbench are included in Chapter 3.

DOUBLE UP.   Make single space do double duty. A laundry room often has possibilities as a shop. A hinged fold-down workbench can go over the washer and dryer. True, a hinged workbench has drawbacks; you have to clear it before you can fold it out of the way. A family recreation room also has shop possibilities. There will be dust and noise, but some families will go along with it.

2

Planning the Layout

You want a shop that is easy to work in, and this can be achieved only by an efficient and logical organization of tools, storage, and work areas. A shop should be organized in centers —everything for a particular function grouped together. If the main function is woodworking, there may be subsidiary areas for planning, painting and finishing, electronics, metalwork, and crafts.

In placing major power tools, the chief considerations are clearance and frequency of use. The most common arrangement is to have a table saw, and perhaps a jointer, in the middle of the shop area. This makes it easier to handle long work, and these tools need clearance on all sides. A radial saw needs clearance on three sides only, so it may be placed against a wall.

Another factor to consider in planning placement of tools is the natural order of their use. Work usually proceeds from storage to cutting to assembly to finishing, just as in a kitchen the sequence is from refrigerator to sink to stove. A well-designed shop should follow this principle.

Placement of the workbench, stationary saw, and storage is most important. Other tools can be placed with a freer hand, provided they have the necessary clearance for safe and comfortable operation. Of course, many major power tools can be placed on retractable casters and moved out for use.

Place hand tools nearest the point of most frequent first use. If tools are used in more than one area of the shop, have duplicates. Point-of-use-storage also makes tools easy to find.

Consider handling of materials. Direct and easy access to the shop from outdoors is the ideal arrangement, but it is not always possible. Ceiling height is important, as you'll discover the first time you try to flop a 12′ board.

Let's look at three shops designed by experts. In a multi-purpose shop created by Hubert Luckett, Editor-in-Chief of *Popular Science* magazine, the woodworking center is focused around four tools: table saw, radial saw, jointer, and belt-disc sander. By concentrating the work area around them, many steps are saved.

These tools are all used in the basic cutting and fitting of parts. Assembly is at a nearby center-island bench. Small tools are stored on wall racks behind panels that drop down to serve as work tables. All benches and tabletops are the same height so they can function as added supports for long work. An extension table, hinged to the wall, folds down so it can serve both the radial and the table saw. Reserving the radial saw for crosscut work, and the table saw for ripping, permits each tool to do the kind of job it handles best, and eliminates changing blades and saw position.

The second major area in the shop is a metalworking center. Drill press, band saw, and bench grinder are grouped here because they are used more for metalworking than for woodworking. Strictly for metalworking are a 9″ metal lathe, a forge, anvil, quench tub, gas and electric welders, and a welding table topped by ½″ boiler plate. A hooded exhaust fan discharges fumes from both forge and welding table. Everything needed for auto work is stored in a roll-about cart.

Multipurpose shop includes areas for woodworking, metalworking, and electronics.

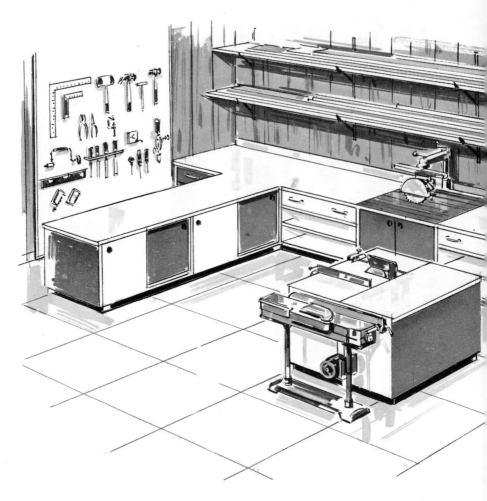

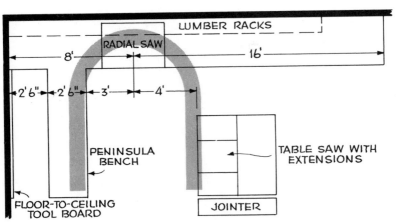

LUMBER RACKS

RADIAL SAW

8'

16'

2' 6" 2' 6" 3' 4'

PENINSULA
BENCH

TABLE SAW WITH
EXTENSIONS

FLOOR-TO-CEILING
TOOL BOARD

JOINTER

U-shaped shop saves steps, can fit in a small basement or single-car garage.

The third major area is an electronics work center. Located in a rear corner, it has an L-shaped rather than a conventional straight bench. A chassis can be tested on either leg of the bench with important testing instruments always in easy view. These instruments are on shelves that run diagonally across the corner.

A U-shaped plan is the most popular in kitchens, and it works extremely well in a shop, too. Everything is always within easy reach. Such a shop, designed by Jackson Hand, well-known expert, has its horseshoe shape formed by a radial saw built into a wall bench, a peninsular bench that extends

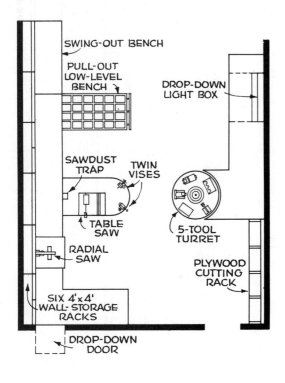

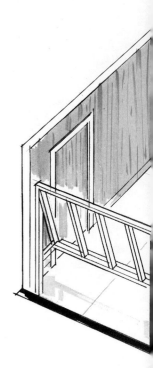

out from it at right angles, and a table saw and jointer on the third side.

Mr. Hand places his radial saw 8' from one end of the bench and 16' from the other. This permits cutting 16-footers at the middle or the ends. Lumber is stored on wall racks just behind the saw, instantly at hand for selection and use. A tool storage board is run from floor to ceiling. It not only concentrates a great variety of tools in one spot, but it eliminates stretching across a bench to get them.

For space saving, several small power tools may be grouped on a revolving turret. A circular turret in a shop designed by former *Popular Science* editor Sheldon M. Gallagher holds a drill press, jigsaw, belt-disc sander, bench grinder, and small shaper. The central pedestal is 3" pipe with a spring latch that locks the turret in any desired position.

Focal point of this shop is the five-tool turret. A quick turn
delivers any tool to your fingertips.

DRAWING PLANS.   It is advisable to draw plans for the shop. You can't keep it all in your head. Once you have something on paper, over a period of time you can incorporate changes as new ideas occur. The plan doesn't have to be fancy, but it should be done to scale. A good scale is ¼" to the foot. If you have trouble keeping lines at right angles, or calculating scale, use graph paper that has ¼" squares. Layout includes more than just a flat floor plan. It must also include what will go on the walls and be suspended from the ceiling.

The first thing to get on paper is the exact space available. Indicate locations of windows, posts, doors, stairs, heating plant.

Make an inventory of your present tools and those you plan to get. You will have to plan a place for each of them. If you can, leave a little extra space for such expansion that may not be foreseeable now.

Tool symbols shown are in ¼" scale. Duplicate them as cardboard cutouts, and you will have a handy means for testing various arrangments. You'll find it easier to move cutouts made this size on your own drawing than to shove the actual tools around on your shop floor site. Each tool has its light and clearance requirements. Provide for them.

When the arrangement of all elements in the shop is set, you will have a basis for deciding where lighting fixtures, power outlets, vacuum system, etc. should go. Remember such needs as a ventilating fan, telephone, intercom, TV outlet, waste bins, possibly a washbasin. If you like to relax to music as you work, provide a place for speakers.

By using a trolley track or lighting duct, you can have light and power anywhere in the shop. Power tools can plug into the track from middle-of-the-floor locations, and it's safer not to have power lines snaking across the floor.

If the workshop is being developed as part of a larger overall improvement project, don't plan it piecemeal. If you are remodeling a basement, and the workshop is only stage one, with a playroom, sewing room, or other facilities to come later,

Long, narrow basement space accommodates woodworking shop and darkroom. Portable tools are stored on shelves under stairway.

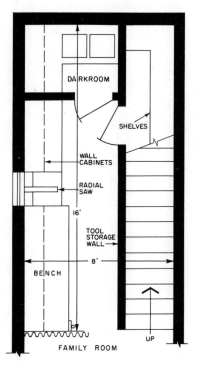

DARKROOM

SHELVES

WALL CABINETS

RADIAL SAW

16'

TOOL STORAGE WALL →

8'

BENCH

UP

FAMILY ROOM

Garage "bustle" shop, 6′ by 15′, is large enough for most jobs. For big woodworking projects, tools are rolled into the garage. Twin storage doors swing open flat against walls, out of the way. Lumber is stored on overhead racks in garage. For added bench space, the lathe may be hinge-mounted to swing up against the wall.

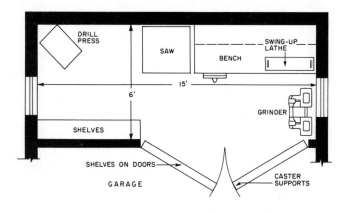

DRILL PRESS

SAW

BENCH

SWING-UP LATHE

15'

6'

SHELVES

GRINDER

SHELVES ON DOORS

GARAGE

CASTER SUPPORTS

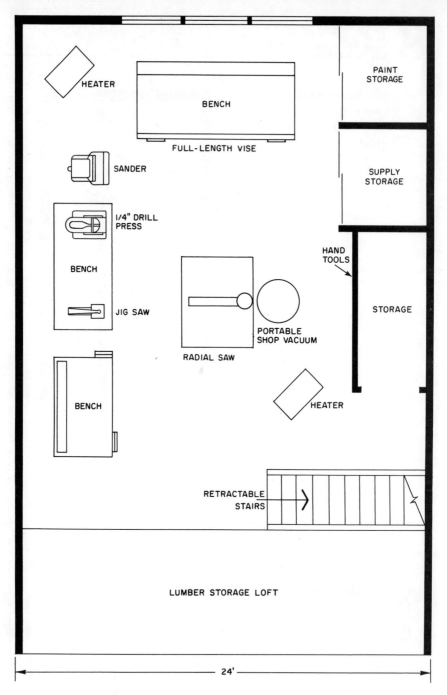

HEATER

BENCH

FULL-LENGTH VISE

SANDER

1/4" DRILL PRESS

BENCH

JIG SAW

BENCH

PAINT STORAGE

SUPPLY STORAGE

HAND TOOLS

STORAGE

PORTABLE SHOP VACUUM

RADIAL SAW

HEATER

RETRACTABLE STAIRS

LUMBER STORAGE LOFT

24'

Attic shop uses low-headroom space on one side for storage, on other for recessing benches and equipment. Radial saw is partially enclosed by hood which connects to portable shop vacuum behind it.

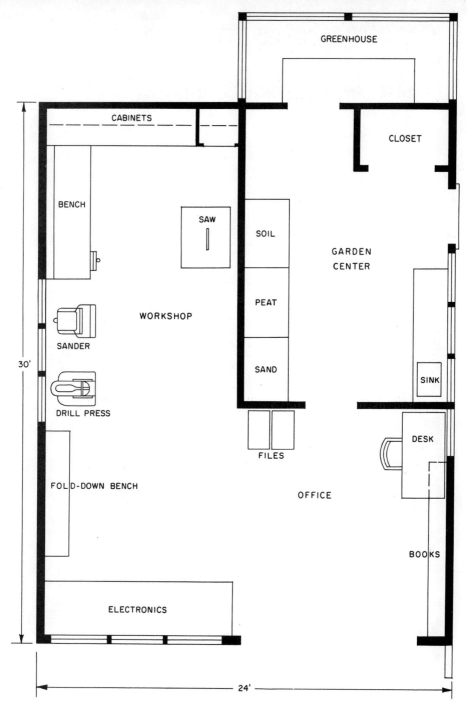

Double garage converted to shop, office, potting room, and greenhouse. One garage-door opening remains to permit passage of large projects and materials.

SPACE AND LIGHT REQUIREMENTS FOR POWER TOOLS

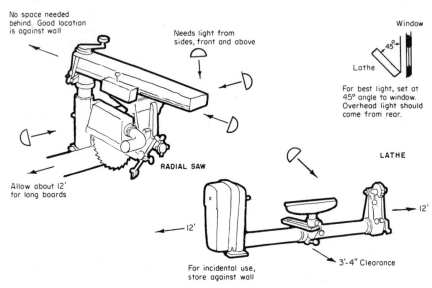

No space needed behind. Good location is against wall

Needs light from sides, front and above

Allow about 12' for long boards

RADIAL SAW

Window

Lathe

45°

For best light, set at 45° angle to window. Overhead light should come from rear.

LATHE

12'

12'

3'-4" Clearance

For incidental use, store against wall

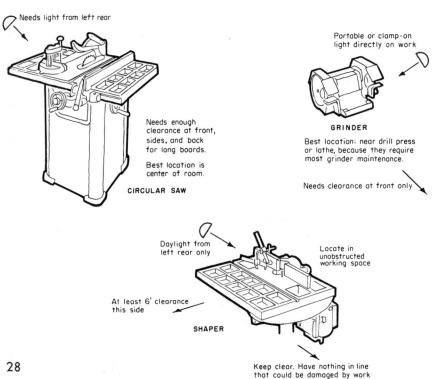

Needs light from left rear

Needs enough clearance at front, sides, and back for long boards.

Best location is center of room.

CIRCULAR SAW

Portable or clamp-on light directly on work

GRINDER

Best location: near drill press or lathe, because they require most grinder maintenance.

Needs clearance at front only

Daylight from left rear only

Locate in unobstructed working space

At least 6' clearance this side

SHAPER

Keep clear. Have nothing in line that could be damaged by work hurled from machine.

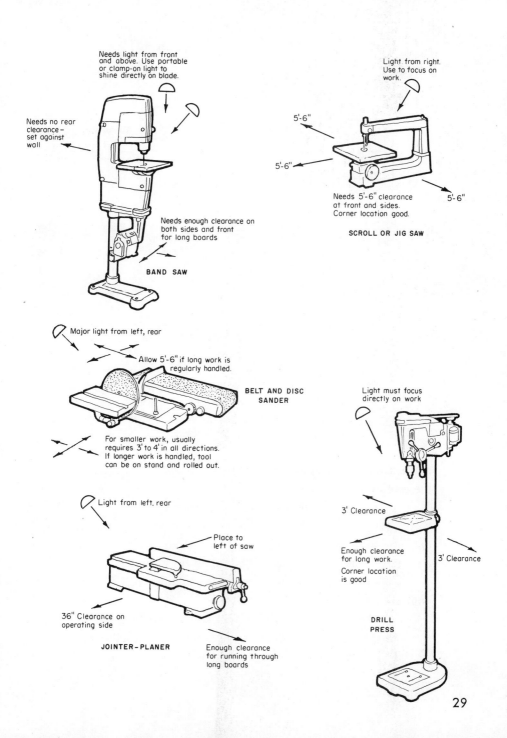

Needs light from front and above. Use portable or clamp-on light to shine directly on blade.

Needs no rear clearance – set against wall

Needs enough clearance on both sides and front for long boards

BAND SAW

Light from right. Use to focus on work.

5'-6"

5'-6"

5'-6"

Needs 5'-6" clearance at front and sides. Corner location good.

SCROLL OR JIG SAW

Major light from left, rear

Allow 5'-6" if long work is regularly handled.

BELT AND DISC SANDER

For smaller work, usually requires 3' to 4' in all directions. If longer work is handled, tool can be on stand and rolled out.

Light from left, rear

Place to left of saw

36" Clearance on operating side

JOINTER-PLANER

Enough clearance for running through long boards

Light must focus directly on work

3' Clearance

Enough clearance for long work.

Corner location is good

3' Clearance

DRILL PRESS

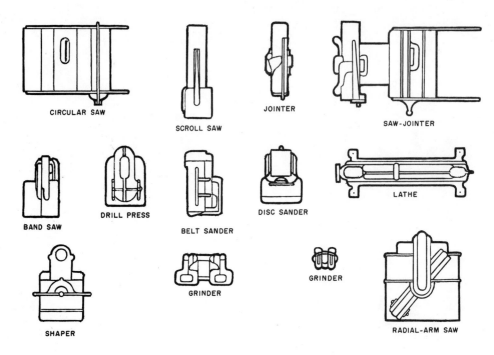

CIRCULAR SAW

SCROLL SAW

JOINTER

SAW-JOINTER

BAND SAW

DRILL PRESS

BELT SANDER

DISC SANDER

LATHE

SHAPER

GRINDER

GRINDER

RADIAL-ARM SAW

These symbols, drawn on a scale of ¼″ to a foot, are the approximate size of power tools you now have or will want for your shop. Trace over them and make handy cutouts to help you visualize various shop layouts. Arrange your cutouts on a plan of your shop site, drawn on a ¼″ to a foot scale and showing the location of windows, posts, stairs, and other permanent features.

make a master plan that will show exactly what is to go into these other areas.

A typical workshop starts small, grows through the years. Every few years it may require reorganization to accommodate new tools, new supplies, and expanded interests. If you are a renter, or on the move, plan your shop for easy disassembly.

To sum up, here are seven rules to follow in planning your shop:

1. Organize each activity with its own work center.
2. Have principal work surfaces the same height.
3. Put large power tools on casters so they can be moved.

4. Provide duplicate hand tools at each place they are needed.
5. Use continuous strip wiring to let you plug in tools anywhere.
6. For safety's sake, provide your shop with adequate lighting.
7. Keep arrangements flexible. Plan for expansion.

3

Workbenches

If there is one indispensable item in a shop it is the bench. You'll spend more time here for most projects and repairs than anywhere else. A shop without a bench is like a kitchen without counter space.

A workbench usually is from 24″ to 30″ wide and from 4′ to 7′ or more long. Height ranges from about 30″ to 34″, depending on how tall you are. The top should be even with your hip joint, to permit you to work without stooping.

A bench should have at least 18″ clearance at each end. If you don't have clearance at an end, you can't work there. If there isn't enough space along one wall for the bench, you can turn the corner with it, but ends should be clear. The corner can have a lazy-susan arrangement under the counter for storage.

Some prefer to place their bench in the center of the shop, giving access from all four sides. Instead of being confined to a small board above the bench, tools can be stored on the entire wall nearby.

A bench must not become a catch-all for tools. Provide space for storage under the bench top. If drawers or cabinets extend to the floor, you won't have the problem of debris collecting underneath.

Don't attach power tools permanently to the bench top, especially a grinder or machinist's vise. The bench top is actually too high for a grinder. Mount the vise on a 9"-by-9"-by-2" block, and when you need the vise, clamp it in place in your wood vise. You'll also find a wood vise handy for holding a sharpening stone. The stone should be mounted in a wood block to protect it from breaking.

Be sure your bench is level lengthwise and crosswise. Your floor may not be level and adjustments may have to be made in the length of the bench legs to compensate for it.

For convenience, provide enough electrical outlets at the bench so that you don't have to string extension cords. The tangle of power-tool cords can also be avoided by using an overhead cord system.

You can start with the bench, add other modular units later to create a complete work center. Bench top is 20" deep, of tough industrial material. Sliding door cabinets, 5" deep, have adjustable shelves. *Courtesy The Hirsh Company.*

Somewhere on the bench nail a yardstick with a stop at its end. It comes in handy for measuring and marking boards for rough cutting.

Haunt the house-wrecker's yards and secondhand shops if you want to pick up the makings of a bargain bench. Old desks and chests need only the addition of a more durable and spacious top to become a workbench with an array of ready-made drawers.

If you prefer to buy a bench, a wide variety is available. The Hirsh Company has modular units that can be used individually, or combined to fit just about any space. More expensive benches, of European manufacture, come knocked down, which saves you money on shipping. They are usually easily assembled with no more than a wrench and screwdriver. Sears, Wards, and J.C. Penney are good mail-order sources for benches.

The pages ahead show you how to make your own.

The new Black & Decker Workmate portable work center, giant vise and sawborse is helpful in getting the job done in many useful ways including (left) a clamp for an irregular or circular object and (right) a vise for a hard to handle piece like a door.

If you buy bench legs, putting your own bench together is no problem whatever. You merely supply the top, shelf, and doors or drawers. Steel legs, by Akro-Mils, are pre-drilled to accommodate doors, drawers, electrical boxes.

Swedish Sjoberg bench, from School Products Co., New York, features dovetail joints and three separate vises. Large lockable cupboard and five drawers provide tool and hardware storage. Made of seasoned beech, pine and birch. Overall length—63″.

FIVE WORKBENCHES
YOU CAN BUILD

1. Beginner's Workbench
2. Lock-Up Workbench
3. Power-Tool Workbench
4. 4-Way Workbench
5. Living-Room Workbench

In the following section are plans for building several practical workbenches, from a simple model that can be constructed in a couple of hours, to more elaborate types that will challenge your skill and provide you with a complete work center when you have finished.

BEGINNER'S WORKBENCH

This simple bench can be built in a short time with only hand tools and will serve as a solid and durable work surface in a small shop. The frame is made of 2-by-4s; the top and shelf of ¾″ plywood; and the back and sides of ¼″ ply. The plywood gives maximum rigidity to the frame. For details on building the tool rack see Chapter 5. *Courtesy American Plywood Assoc.*

Plans for Building
the Beginner's Workbench

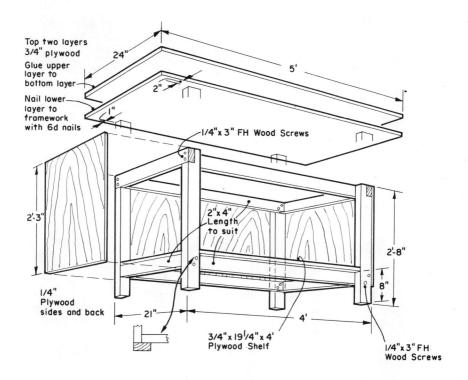

Top two layers 3/4" plywood

Glue upper layer to bottom layer

Nail lower layer to framework with 6d nails

24"

5'

2"

1"

1/4"x 3" FH Wood Screws

2'-3"

2"x 4" Length to suit

2'-8"

8"

1/4" Plywood sides and back

21"

4'

3/4"x 19¼"x 4' Plywood Shelf

1/4"x3"FH Wood Screws

3/4" Plywood. BD Cutting Diagram

Shelf | Top

Top

First step in building the bench is to draw cutting diagrams on ¾″ and ¼″ plywood panels using a straightedge and square. Then mark the pieces (sides, back, etc.) and cut them out, allowing for saw kerfs.

Cut all 2-by-4s, notching one end of each leg; drill screw holes; and assemble the two end frames with glue and screws. Countersink screw holes for best results.

Nail and glue the side panel to one end frame, then join the two end frames with long 2-by-4s, using glue and screws. Other side panel goes on after shelf's in place.

Insert lower shelf through open end frame and glue and nail it in place. Then glue and nail lower top panel to the top rails. Glue the top panel to the lower panel and keep under pressure until dry. This eliminates screws or nails in the bench top and gives a smooth finish.

LOCK-UP
WORKBENCH

This workbench allows you to keep tools locked behind sliding doors, protected against rust and the curious hands of children. The ¾" plywood side panels support a husky top of glued-up 1¾" hardwood strips. Fluorescent lamps behind the valance supply excellent illumination, and an outlet strip along the front of the bench provides connections for power tools at point of use. In this version, a pullout storage shelf for portable power tools was installed in one bottom cabinet; the other was left open for storage.

Plans for Building
the Lock-up Workbench

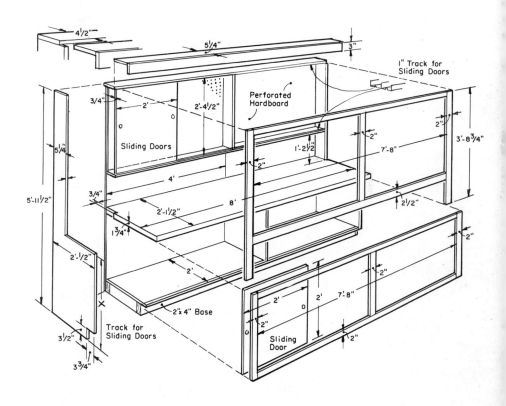

Measurement "X" on the side panels is optional, depending on the height of the user.

POWER-TOOL
WORKBENCH

Here's a workbench designed especially for hand power
tools. The tools are stored in a locked cabinet, and are
equipped with quick-disconnect fittings which plug into a
single overhead cord that winds up when not in use. The
unit features a 4'-long stand-up bench with tool chest; a
smaller work table with a pullout bench for sitting or
sawing; and a storage shelf for bulky items.

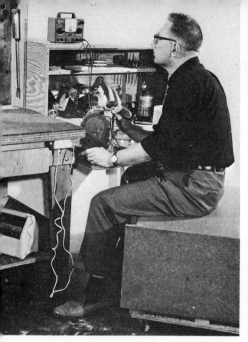

Door of tool cabinet, supported by a hinged leg, serves as a work table (left), the rolling bench as a stool, or a platform for cutting panels (right).

Frame of 2-by-6s is assembled first. After building the two sides, attach the rear rail and the left rear leg; then add the front rail.

Turn the bench upside down after adding the bench top and tool cabinet. This makes it easy to install the drawer runners, lower rear rail, and bottom shelf.

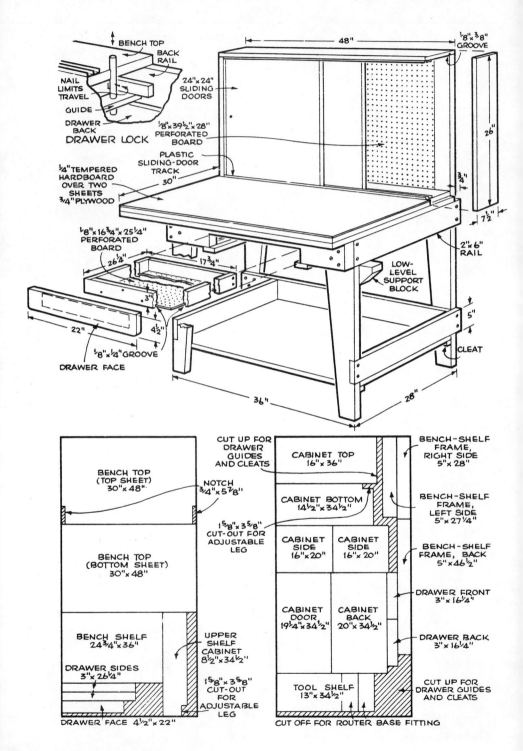

BENCH TOP

BACK RAIL

NAIL LIMITS TRAVEL

GUIDE

DRAWER BACK

DRAWER LOCK

24"x 24" SLIDING DOORS

⅛"x 39½"x 28" PERFORATED BOARD

PLASTIC SLIDING-DOOR TRACK

¼" TEMPERED HARDBOARD OVER TWO SHEETS ¾" PLYWOOD

30"

⅛"x 16¾"x 25¼" PERFORATED BOARD

26¼"

17¾"

3"

22"

4½"

⅛"x ¼" GROOVE

DRAWER FACE

LOW-LEVEL SUPPORT BLOCK

2"x 6" RAIL

5"

CLEAT

36"

28"

48"

⅛"x ⅜" GROOVE

26"

¾"

7½"

BENCH TOP (TOP SHEET) 30"x 48"

NOTCH ¾"x 5⅞"

BENCH TOP (BOTTOM SHEET) 30"x 48"

BENCH SHELF 24¾"x 36"

DRAWER SIDES 3"x 26¼"

UPPER SHELF CABINET 8½"x 34½"

1⅝"x 3⅝" CUT-OUT FOR ADJUSTABLE LEG

DRAWER FACE 4½"x 22"

CUT UP FOR DRAWER GUIDES AND CLEATS

CABINET TOP 16"x 36"

CABINET BOTTOM 14½"x 34½"

1⅝"x 3⅝" CUT-OUT FOR ADJUSTABLE LEG

CABINET SIDE 16"x 20"

CABINET SIDE 16"x 20"

CABINET DOOR 19¼"x 34½"

CABINET BACK 20"x 34½"

TOOL SHELF 13"x 34½"

CUT OFF FOR ROUTER BASE FITTING

BENCH-SHELF FRAME, RIGHT SIDE 5"x 28"

BENCH-SHELF FRAME, LEFT SIDE 5"x 27¼"

BENCH-SHELF FRAME, BACK 5"x 46½"

DRAWER FRONT 3"x 16¼"

DRAWER BACK 3"x 16¼"

CUT UP FOR DRAWER GUIDES AND CLEATS

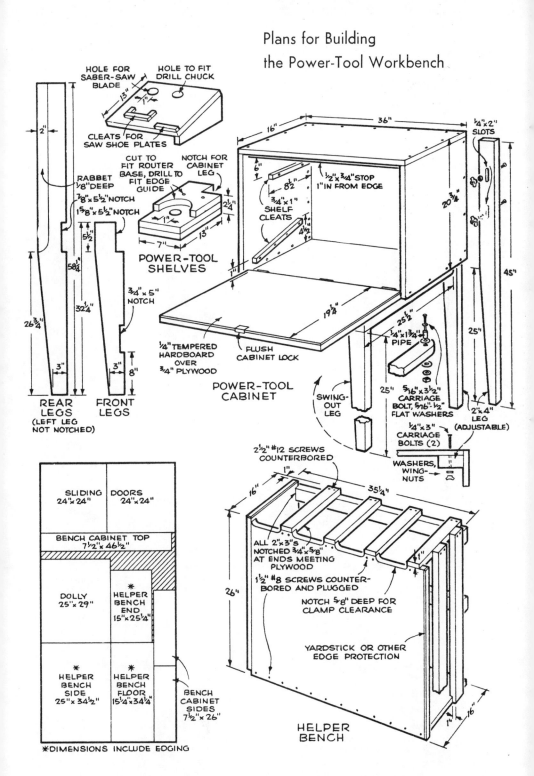

Plans for Building
the Power-Tool Workbench

HOLE FOR
SABER-SAW
BLADE

HOLE TO FIT
DRILL CHUCK

13"

1"

CLEATS FOR
SAW SHOE PLATES

2"

RABBET
1/8" DEEP

1/8" x 5 1/2" NOTCH

1 5/8" x 5 1/2" NOTCH

CUT TO
FIT ROUTER
BASE, DRILL TO
FIT EDGE
GUIDE

NOTCH FOR
CABINET
LEG

2 1/4"
1/4"

7"

13"

1"

POWER-TOOL
SHELVES

5 1/2"

58 1/4"

32 1/4"

3/4" x 5"
NOTCH

26 3/4"

3"

3"

8"

REAR
LEGS
(LEFT LEG
NOT NOTCHED)

FRONT
LEGS

1/4" TEMPERED
HARDBOARD
OVER
3/4" PLYWOOD

FLUSH
CABINET LOCK

POWER-TOOL
CABINET

36"

16"

1/4" x 2"
SLOTS

6"

8 1/2"

1/2" x 3/4" STOP
1" IN FROM EDGE

3/4" x 1"
SHELF
CLEATS

4 1/2"

20 3/4"

1"

19 1/4"

45"

25 1/2"

1/4" x 1 3/4"
PIPE

25"

25"

5/16" x 3 1/2"
CARRIAGE
BOLT, 5/16"- 1/2"
FLAT WASHERS

2"x 4"
LEG
(ADJUSTABLE)

SWING-
OUT
LEG

1/4" x 3"
CARRIAGE
BOLTS (2)

WASHERS,
WING-
NUTS

SLIDING 24"x 24"	DOORS 24"x 24"
BENCH CABINET TOP 7 1/2" x 46 1/2"	
DOLLY 25"x 29"	* HELPER BENCH END 15"x25 1/4"
* HELPER BENCH SIDE 25"x 34 1/2"	* HELPER BENCH FLOOR 15 1/4"x34 3/4"

BENCH
CABINET
SIDES
7 1/2"x 26"

*DIMENSIONS INCLUDE EDGING

2 1/2" #12 SCREWS
COUNTERBORED

1"

16"

35 1/4"

ALL 2"x 3"S
NOTCHED 3/4"x 5/8"
AT ENDS MEETING
PLYWOOD

1 1/2" #8 SCREWS COUNTER-
BORED AND PLUGGED

NOTCH 5/8" DEEP FOR
CLAMP CLEARANCE

YARDSTICK OR OTHER
EDGE PROTECTION

26"

1"

16"

HELPER
BENCH

4-WAY
WORKBENCH

This sleek workbench conceals a couple of surprises. In addition to its ample work surface, it contains a lathe, and a scrap bin that doubles as a bench for sawing and gluing.

Scrap bin with hinged framework top makes use of ordinarily wasted space.

Pulled onto the floor, the scrap bin serves as a support for sawing and gluing. It can be rolled on its casters to other parts of the shop.

Hinged bench top swings up, revealing the lathe stored
sideways inside.

Lathe is pulled into position with a sturdy lever. The
hinged platform on which the lathe is mounted swings up,
pushing up rear flap, which then slips under it and acts as
a brace.

Plans for Building
the 4-Way Workbench

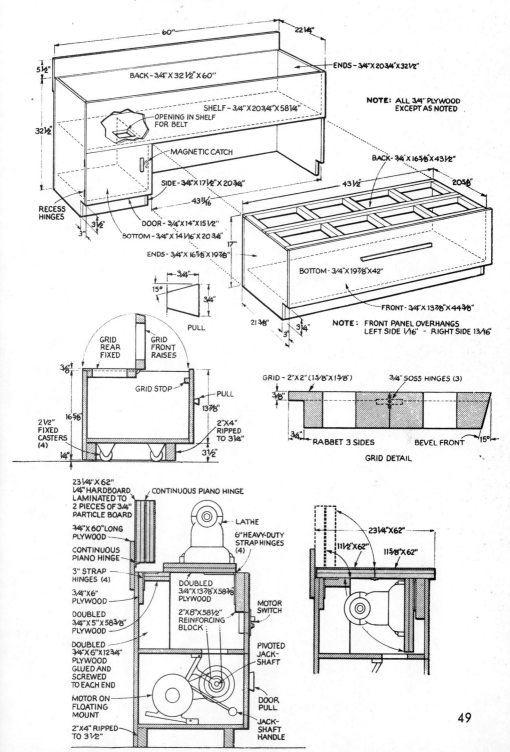

BACK – 3/4" X 32 1/2" X 60"

60"

22 1/4"

ENDS – 3/4" X 20 3/4" X 32 1/2"

5 1/2"

32 1/2"

SHELF – 3/4" X 20 3/4" X 58 1/4"

OPENING IN SHELF
FOR BELT

NOTE: ALL 3/4" PLYWOOD
EXCEPT AS NOTED

MAGNETIC CATCH

BACK – 3/4" X 16 5/8" X 43 1/2"

SIDE – 3/4" X 17 1/2" X 20 3/4"

43 1/2"

20 5/8"

RECESS
HINGES

43 11/16"

DOOR – 3/4" X 14" X 15 1/2"

BOTTOM – 3/4" X 14 1/16" X 20 3/4"

3"

3 1/2"

ENDS – 3/4" X 16 5/8" X 19 7/8"

17"

BOTTOM – 3/4" X 19 7/8" X 42"

3/4"

15°

3/4"

PULL

FRONT – 3/4" X 13 7/8" X 44 3/8"

21 3/8"

3 1/4"

3"

NOTE: FRONT PANEL OVERHANGS
LEFT SIDE 1/16" – RIGHT SIDE 13/16"

GRID
REAR
FIXED

GRID
FRONT
RAISES

3/8"

GRID STOP

PULL

2 1/2"
FIXED
CASTERS
(4)

16 5/8"

13 7/8"

2"X4"
RIPPED
TO 3 1/4"

1/4"

3 1/2"

GRID – 2"X2" (1 5/8" X 1 5/8")

3/4" SOSS HINGES (3)

3/8"

3/4"

RABBET 3 SIDES

BEVEL FRONT

15°

GRID DETAIL

23 1/4" X 62"
1/4" HARDBOARD
LAMINATED TO
2 PIECES OF 3/4"
PARTICLE BOARD

CONTINUOUS PIANO HINGE

LATHE

3/4" X 60" LONG
PLYWOOD

6" HEAVY-DUTY
STRAP HINGES
(4)

CONTINUOUS
PIANO HINGE

DOUBLED
3/4" X 13 7/8" X 58 3/8"
PLYWOOD

3" STRAP
HINGES (4)

3/4" X 6"
PLYWOOD

2"X8" X 58 1/2"
REINFORCING
BLOCK

MOTOR
SWITCH

DOUBLED
3/4" X 5" X 58 3/8"
PLYWOOD

DOUBLED
3/4" X 6" X 12 3/4"
PLYWOOD
GLUED AND
SCREWED
TO EACH END

PIVOTED
JACK-
SHAFT

MOTOR ON
FLOATING
MOUNT

2"X4" RIPPED
TO 3 1/2"

DOOR
PULL

JACK-
SHAFT
HANDLE

23 1/4" X 62"

11 1/2" X 62"

11 5/8" X 62"

49

LIVING-ROOM
WORKBENCH

Handsome cabinet looks like a respectable piece of furniture, but it's actually a complete workshop. Hinged top opens to display ample assortment of hand tools (right).

Narrow panel on front of cabinet hinges up and work table slides out, supported by screw-on legs that are stored in the interior. The inner sides of the cabinet doors hold bits, blades, sandpaper, and fastenings.

With doors open, a drawer on heavy-duty slides pulls out. It holds planes, hand brace, clamps, metal cutters, etc.

Portable power tools fit into holes cut in a ½″ plywood shelf at the front of the cabinet bottom.

Frame holds plastic sheeting over workbench for controlling sawdust when sanding. Holes in plastic reinforced with masking tape provide access for hands and electric cord from power sander.

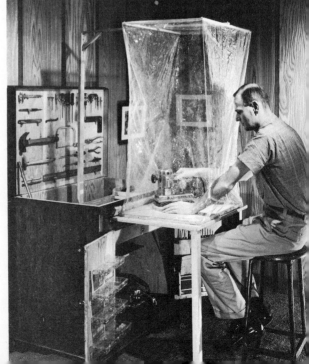

Plans for Building
the Living-Room Workbench

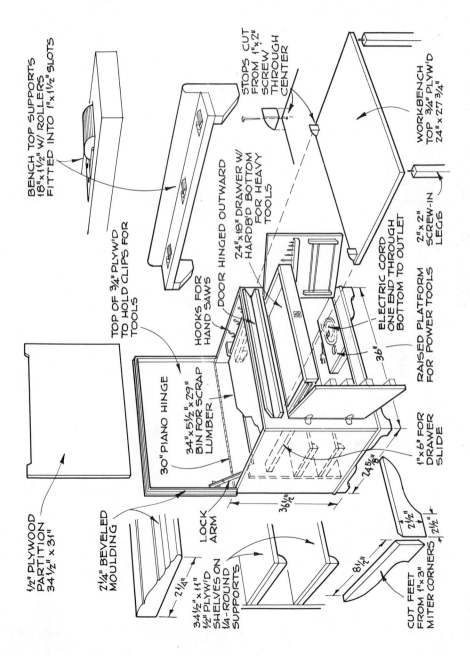

BENCH TOP SUPPORTS 18"x1 1/2" W/ ROLLERS FITTED INTO 1"x1 1/2" SLOTS

STOPS CUT FROM 1"x 2" SCREW THROUGH CENTER

WORKBENCH TOP 3/4" PLYW'D 24"x 27 3/4"

TOP OF 3/4" PLYW'D TO HOLD CLIPS FOR TOOLS

HOOKS FOR HAND SAWS

DOOR HINGED OUTWARD

24"x18" DRAWER W/ HARDB'D BOTTOM FOR HEAVY TOOLS

2"x 2" SCREW-IN LEGS

ELECTRIC CORD ONE END THROUGH BOTTOM TO OUTLET

RAISED PLATFORM FOR POWER TOOLS

36"

30" PIANO HINGE

34"x 5 1/2"x 29" BIN FOR SCRAP LUMBER

1"x6" FOR DRAWER SLIDE

14 1/2"

8"

36 1/2"

1/2" PLYWOOD PARTITION 34 1/2" x 31"

2 1/4" BEVELED MOULDING

LOCK ARM

34 1/2"x 11" 1/2" PLYW'D SHELVES ON 1/4-ROUND SUPPORTS

2 1/4"

8 1/2"

CUT FEET FROM 1"x 3" MITER CORNERS

2 1/2"

2 1/2"

4

Shop Construction

WORKSHOP WALLS. All basements and many garages are of masonry construction. If these areas are used for a shop, their walls require special treatment to keep them from getting damp and cold. Basement walls may get damp because of seepage from outside, or because of moisture condensation on their cool surface during hot, humid weather.

If seepage is from outside, first check to see that rainfall is diverted away from the walls. If the ground does not slope away from the walls, regrade so that it does. Lead the water from downspouts away from the house, either to storm sewers or to sloping runoff areas.

After heavy rainstorms, check for points where water is entering and mark them with a grease pencil. The most frequent point of entry is a crack where walls meet floor. Squeegee or sponge-mop water away to create a dry spot; then you can trace the location of the leak.

Cracks and holes through which water is entering can be immediately plugged with hydraulic cement. Follow the manufacturer's directions. Regular patcher is easier to use. If you can wait until walls dry out, you'll do a more satisfactory job.

Block walls are porous. To seal them against seepage, after active holes and cracks have been plugged, coat walls with at least two coats of scrubbed-in powder-type block filler and sealer. Special brushes are available for the purpose. The kind with a handle is easiest to use. Follow manufacturer's instructions. A tank-type garden sprayer is good for fogging the walls with moisture. Walls should be damp but not wet.

When basement walls and floors are subjected to water under pressure, the pressure can be relieved and the basement secured against flooding by the installation of an automatic sump pump. To install a pump, first recess into the floor a section of clay sewer pipe 16″ to 24″ in diameter and 2′ to 4′ long. The pump is set into this pit. Install a pipe from the pump to take the discharge from this sump either to a point of runoff outside the house or to a sewer. If the pipe is connected to the sewer, a check valve must be used to prevent backflow. The pump, plugged into an ordinary electrical outlet, will come on automatically whenever the water level rises in the sump. In some cases it is necessary to jackhammer trenches in the floor around the wall perimeter, and crossing the floor, and install drain tiles leading to the sump.

Masonry walls tend to be cold. Your body radiates heat to these cold surfaces and you feel chilled even though the air temperature may register 72 degrees. To avoid this radiant-heat loss, warm up basement walls by covering them with paneling, either boards or sheet material.

Basements that are subjected to water under pressure can be made safe and dry by installing a sump pump. Plugged into an ordinary electric outlet, the pump will come on automatically whenever the water level rises in the sump.

Some manufacturers recommend vertical furring strips for attaching paneling, others horizontal. Furring can be attached to masonry walls with special adhesive, and panels attached to the furring with the same adhesive. Tapping panels with a padded block insures adhesion.

Paneling pointers. Paneling is applied over 1″-by-2″ furring strips which can be attached to masonry with a special adhesive available at your building supply dealer. They can be fastened to block walls by driving spiral nails into mortar joints, but do this only where there is no danger that nail holes will cause leakage.

Place furring strips horizontally, 16″ apart, measured from the center of one strip to the center of the next. When using 4′-by-8′ panels, also apply furring strips 48″ on centers vertically to correspond to panel joints. Allow ¼″ space where vertical and horizontal furring strips meet. If walls are uneven, level out furring strips by placing flat wood wedges at low spots. Pieces of cedar shingles are ideal for the purpose.

Before applying paneling, staple vapor-barrier paper or polyethylene film over the furring strips to prevent moisture from penetrating.

Sheet material can be applied to the furring strips with adhesive, or can be nailed. All four edges of each panel should be attached to the furring. There should be no "floating" edges.

Start paneling in a corner of the room. To achieve a perfect fit at out-of-plumb corners and around projections, place the panel in position and with a pair of compasses scribe

In some cases, as in a garage, it may be desirable to insulate masonry before applying paneling. Use 2"-by-2" furring strips to allow for thickness of insulation.

a line from the top of the panel to the bottom, with one leg of the compass following the wall and the other on the panel. Cut along the line with a coping or saber saw. To get a neat fit where panels intersect, bevel their edges slightly toward the rear with a plane.

When applying tongue-and-groove board paneling, start at a corner after scribing and face-nail the board at top and bottom. Use galvanized finishing nails 1½" long. The tongue of the board should be facing away from the corner. Subsequent boards are nailed at an angle through the tongues. Continually check the plumb of boards as you nail. Stop the paneling ¼" short of floor and ceiling to allow ventilation from behind. Where humidity conditions are excessive and

These 16"-wide Marlite planks have tongue-and-groove joints which conceal all fastenings.

Tongue-and-groove boards provide an inexpensive and attractive finish to a basement shop. Here the boards are being nailed to studs set on 24″ centers, and nailed to each other at an angle through the tongues.

there is a possibility of condensation on walls even after paneling is applied, install midget louvers every 6″ along the floor and ceiling.

Basement walls may be covered with gypsum wallboard if it is the kind that is backed with foil. The foil prevents vapor from penetrating the wallboard.

In some cases, 2″-by-3″ studs are a more desirable support than furring strips for paneling. If walls are irregular, studs are much easier to plumb. They also make it easier to frame around pipes and other obstructions. There is more space behind a stud wall in which to place wiring. A stud wall need be fastened at only the floor and the ceiling joists overhead. If joists run parallel to the wall, bridge the space in between with a 2-by-3 every 4′. Anchor the floor 2-by-3s with concrete nails. If the concrete is too hard to nail into, use lead anchors set in ¼″ holes about 1½″ deep, or use adhesive. Sight along studs to be sure they are straight before you put them in the wall. If they are crooked, discard them, or use them where it doesn't matter. A bowed stud means a bowed wall.

Frame around water, gas, and electric meters, but when you apply paneling, provide small doors for access. If there is a shut-off on a pipe, provide either a small door or a sliding panel.

Partitions.   There are advantages in dividing a basement. You may wish to use only part of the basement for the
shop. Dividing helps keep noise and dust from spreading. And
it makes it easier to lock the shop, a safety factor where children are concerned.

If you are taking half of a double garage as a shop, partitioning will make the shop area easier to insulate and give
it more wall space. When partitioning an attic, you don't have
to finish all of it if you only need part for your shop.

In many cases, because a partition wall is self-supporting,
a minimum of framework is required. If you use V-joint
tongue-and-groove boards, usually 1"-by-6" in size, and install
them vertically, you need 2"-by-4" studs no closer than on 12'
centers. Boards are nailed to a 2"-by-4" plate attached to the
floor with adhesive, and to a 2-by-4 nailed to the ceiling joists. If
the partition runs parallel to the ceiling joists, locate it directly
under one of them.

To determine how many square feet of boarding you need
for your partition, calculate the wall area and then add 25 percent. If the wall is to receive paint or stain, apply it before
boards are nailed in place. Then when they dry out and shrink,

Partitioning a basement or attic can provide room for a
workshop. Partition studs are placed on 16" centers and
nailed to 2-by-4s at floor and ceiling (right).

Perforated hardboard is an excellent material for creating partitions in shops, and may be applied on only one side of a stud wall. When nailing panels to studs (below) use spacers so holes over stud are saved for hanging tools.

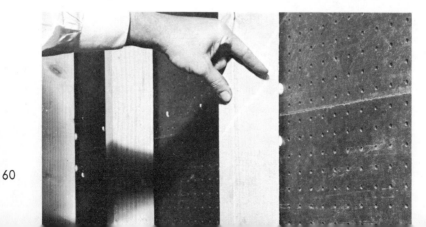

you won't have raw wood showing where the tongues become exposed.

If boards cut off necessary light and air, make your partition of metal mesh. This low-cost material comes in rolls 24″ wide and 50′ long, galvanized or coated with colorful plastic.

Perforated hardboard, commonly known as Peg-Board, is a most popular wall and partition material for shops. In applying it, use fiber spacers to offset the panels ¼″ from the surface. Otherwise holes for hooks and other fixtures will be blocked.

A 4′-by-8′ panel of hardboard will expand ³⁄₁₆″ across its width and ⅜″ in length. Keep the panels where they are to be used for a few days and they'll expand to the normal moisture content of the area. To take care of additional expansion you need leave only about ¹⁄₁₆″ space between panels and at sides.

Hardboard is available in prefinished attractive colors. You can use solid hardboard panels in some areas and matching perforated ones in others. Hardboard, in both the ⅛″ and ¼″ thicknesses, makes good sliding door panels for cabinets. You can get tracks for these panels at your lumberyard.

In an attic, build the walls under the sloping roof far enough out so that they are at least 4′6″ high. The space under the eaves can be used for storage. This is a good place for sliding-door cabinets.

In finishing off the attic, don't obstruct eave louvers that provide ventilation. If you install a flat ceiling under the roof peak, there should be a ventilating louver at each gable end.

Attic partition walls should be built of 2″-by-4″ studs on 16″ centers. Studs are nailed to a 2″-by-4″ sill set flat on the floor and to a 2″-by-4″ cap at the ceiling level. Use double studs on either side of a door opening.

Plasterboard, also known as gypsum wallboard, is one of the least expensive raw materials. Get the ½″ size for maximum rigidity and sound control. For top noise absorption, you can install sound-deadening board as a base for it. This board is ½″ thick and comes in 4′-by-8′ panels. For best results, wallboard should be attached with adhesive to the sound-deadening board.

Gypsum wallboard is available surfaced with vinyl in a choice of colors. It can be cleaned with soap and water. It can be cemented in place or nailed with color-matching nails.

Where added insulation is a critical factor, install mineral wool insulation blankets between the studs. Staple the edges to the studs or wall with vapor barrier toward the warm side of the room. Then nail on a finish wall of $1/2''$ gypsum board or paneling.

CEILINGS.   The best kind of ceiling in a basement is a suspended one. It is also the easiest to put up. As a special advantage, it gives you access to any plumbing pipes and heating ducts that may be covered.

In a typical installation, you just nail or screw wall angles around the perimeter of the shop space at the height you want the new ceiling. Usually you must allow at least 3" between the framework and the lowest part of the old ceiling so that you can insert panels. But you can get one variety that installs without any appreciable loss of headroom.

In addition to the perimeter angles, other supports are hung 2' apart at right angles to the joists. Crosspieces between these supports complete the framework. You lay the panels on the framework and the job is done.

Ceiling panels are 2'-by-2' or 2'-by-4' in size and have a variety of surface finishes, usually vinyl. Generally made of fiberglass or other acoustical material, the panels don't prevent sound from going through to the floor above, but they do keep most of the sounds that strike their surface from bouncing back at you.

In a suspended ceiling, you can combine translucent panels with the acoustical ones and install lights behind them. Used with fluorescent fixtures, the translucent panels diffuse the light and reduce glare. They come in a variety of styles. Some are white vinyl with prism or grid designs; others are of polystyrene.

Suspended ceiling is an excellent overhead finish for a basement shop. Metal supports are fastened around the perimeter of the basement wall; then cross supports are suspended by wire from screw-eyes in the joists.

Lightweight 2′-by-4′ ceiling panels are simply laid in place in the metal grids. They are easily removed for access to concealed plumbing, heating, and wiring.

If there is no headroom to spare in the basement, an acoustical ceiling can be applied to 1″-by-2″ furring strips nailed to the joists. It's important that furring strips be straight, not wavy. Wedge-shaped pieces of shingle driven under strips can remedy irregularities. The tiles are attached to furring strips with a staple gun (right).

For nonsuspended ceilings, you can get acoustical tiles in 12″ and 16″ squares. These can be applied by stapling to furring strips. You can borrow a stapler where you buy the tiles.

For stapling tiles to a gypsum wallboard ceiling there are special "piggy-back" staples. The first staple toes in, the piggy-back staple flares out, providing needed holding power.

You can also install tiles by slipping them, without nailing or stapling, into special angled metal strips that you attach to joists or an existing ceiling.

FLOORS. A concrete floor in a garage or basement is a durable shop surface, but it is strictly utilitarian. You can make it more attractive with paint or tile.

Before painting a floor, it must be cleaned. First, use latex concrete patcher to repair any holes or cracks. Then, clean and degrease the floor with trisodium phosphate or any other cleaner made specifically for concrete.

If the floor has a hard fiinish, to achieve a good bond it may be necessary to etch it. Muriatic acid is a good etching solution. First, scrub the surface with a solution of 1 part concentrated muriatic acid and 3 parts water, using a stiff fiber brush. (*Caution:* Muriatic acid is corrosive. Mix in a glass or polyethylene container, wear rubber gloves when applying it, and don't spatter on clothes or furniture.)

Allow about 1 gallon of solution to each 100 square feet of surface. Let it remain until all bubbling stops and then flush it off thoroughly with plain water. If the surface has not dried uniformly within a few hours it means that some of the acid still remains, so flush it again.

The floor will dry in several hours, depending upon the porosity of the surface, or it may take a day or more. As soon as it is completely dry, you can paint it.

Use a paint specially made for concrete. Some of the best are latex paints. Easiest application is with a 9″ floor roller with a 40″ handle.

Water can rise through cracks in a basement floor. First step in repairing the leak is to chisel out the cracks to a depth of ½″.

Patch the chiseled-out crack with cement mixed with latex. Follow the manufacturer's directions for mixing patching material.

Most common point where water enters is at the joint between floor and wall. Chisel out the weak mortar and apply patching compound.

The toughest finish for concrete is epoxy enamel. It is expensive but long-lasting. Whichever floor finish you use, follow the manufacturer's directions exactly.

Halfway between a paint and a tile is seamless floor covering made of a clear acrylic or urethane plastic in which colorful plastic or metal chips are suspended. It is applied over a base coat that goes on like paint. On this base coat, the plastic is applied. While the plastic is wet, color chips are spread over its surface. Another coat of plastic goes over the top of the flakes and then a final finish coat. The result is a floor that never needs waxing, and because it has no dirt-catching cracks is extremely easy to maintain.

> To provide a smooth base for a tile floor in an attic, nail 4'-by-4' underlayment panels to the rough subfloor with cement-coated nails.

The best kind of tile floor for a shop, whether it goes over concrete or wood, is vinyl asbestos tile. It is low in cost, attractive, and easy to maintain. Avoid tile thinner than $\frac{1}{16}''$. The thicker the tile, the less chance floor irregularities will "ghost through."

The best adhesive for vinyl asbestos tile rolls on and dries clear. Another variety dries black. It is less expensive, but there is a problem of black smudges. For installing vinyl asbestos tile over a radiant-heated floor, there is a special vinyl adhesive. When installing tile over strip wood floors, duplex lining felt is laid first. It has its own special adhesive.

Good system for installing floor tiles is to divide a room into approximate quarters by snapping chalk lines at right angles to each other. A "dry run" placement of tiles will show you where to place lines to minimize cutting. Some flooring tiles are self-stick. Photo by the makers of Armstrong flooring.

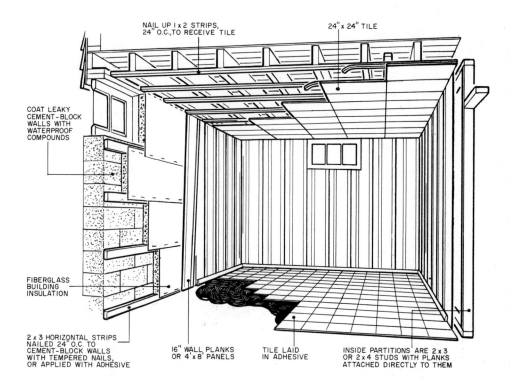

NAIL UP I x 2 STRIPS, 24" O.C.,TO RECEIVE TILE

24" x 24" TILE

COAT LEAKY CEMENT-BLOCK WALLS WITH WATERPROOF COMPOUNDS

FIBERGLASS BUILDING INSULATION

2 x 3 HORIZONTAL STRIPS NAILED 24" O.C. TO CEMENT-BLOCK WALLS WITH TEMPERED NAILS, OR APPLIED WITH ADHESIVE

16" WALL PLANKS OR 4'x 8' PANELS

TILE LAID IN ADHESIVE

INSIDE PARTITIONS ARE 2 x 3 OR 2 x 4 STUDS WITH PLANKS ATTACHED DIRECTLY TO THEM

All the components for finishing a basement are included in this drawing. Horizontal strips of 2-by-3s are used here as backing for fiberglass insulation and wood paneling. Acoustical ceiling tiles are stapled to 1"-by-2" strips; the floor tiles are laid in adhesive. One wall is a partition framed of studs and covered with paneling.

To provide a base for tile over an attic subfloor, underlayment panels are required. These come in 4'-by-4' sheets, slightly less than ¼" thick. They are nailed down with cement-coated nails every 6" on lines 6" apart.

In ordering floor tile, allow about 10 percent extra for waste. If the floor is uneven, use special leveling compound available where you buy the tile.

You can buy in kit form everything you need for a tile installation—a disposable roller, an adhesive scoop, a sharp cutting knife, and a 25' chalk line.

STAIRS.   Direct access from the shop to outdoors is invaluable. You don't have to go through the house to get to the shop, and moving lumber and other materials is simplified. It is especially important in a basement shop.

Creating a new entrance to the basement from outdoors requires digging out the earth at the point the stairway is to be installed and breaking through the masonry basement wall. The excavated well, typically 4′ wide and 5′ long, is lined with walls of masonry block or poured concrete, on a poured

New entrance to a basement shop was created here by digging a well and lining it with poured concrete. Stair stringer was cut from 2″ lumber, but steel stringers are available which can be nailed to the side walls and fitted with wood treads.

These basement stairs contain ample storage area underneath, closed off by hinged doors of tongue-and-groove knotty pine. Minimum headroom for a stairway is 6′6″.

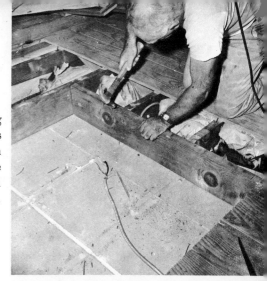

Installing a disappearing stairway in an attic requires cutting joists to make an opening. Joists must then be reinforced by a header nailed to the ends and those at sides.

If there is sufficient headroom in the attic, you can make your own disappearing stairway. Counterweight makes it easy to move stairway up and down in sliding track of 2-by-2s (below). Stringers and treads are cut from 2-by-8s.

concrete base a minimum of 3½" thick. If the well is to be covered by an all-steel door, make it a size that will fit the units available in your area. Steel stair-stringers are available which can be nailed to the side walls of the well. Treads of 2"-by-10" lumber can then be tapped into the stair slots with a hammer. For the entry through the basement wall, you can buy an exterior door frame complete with sill. A door 3' wide is recommended.

If there are no stairs leading to your attic or the loft above your garage, the simplest solution is a folding stairway. A spring mechanism does most of the work of folding and unfolding. Get the largest size that will fit your available space.

If there is no hatchway to the attic space where the stairway is to be placed, you will have to cut one. This may require cutting one or more joists. Support the cut ends with doubled headers made of the same stock as the joists. Nail the headers securely to joists on each side as well as to the cut-off ends.

INSULATION.   In an attic, or in a frame garage with exposed studding, the easiest kind of insulation to install is a type of fiberglass that requires no stapling. It comes in preformed batts and fits by friction. Push it into the stud spaces and it stays there. Use 3" thickness in walls, 6" in ceilings or roof areas.

All insulation requires a vapor barrier on its interior or warm side. With friction-fit fiberglass, use 2-mil polyethylene film. You can get it 8' wide, which means an almost complete elimination of joints.

In places where batt insulation can't be used, try pour-type fiberglass or vermiculite. You can rake it between attic joists to any depth desired.

On masonry walls in basement or garage you can use urethane panels. Urethane is one of the best insulators known. Apply furring strips at top, bottom, and between the ¾"-thick panels. So that the furring strips can serve as nailers for wall finish applied after the insulation is in place, trim the 4'-by-8'

Preformed bats of fiberglass insulation fit between attic stud space and require no stapling. Ventilation is provided by triangular louver which fits at roof peak where hot air would otherwise collect.

insulation panels 1½″ on one side and end to allow for the width of the furring strips.

BUILDING AN EXTENSION. An easy kind of shop to build is a lean-to against the house or garage. The existing structure serves as one wall and you have only three to add.

The lean-to should be located on a "non-bearing" wall. This is a wall on which the existing roof rafters do not rest. When you saw an opening in this wall, cut studs so that you can bridge the opening with a 4″-by-8″ header (two 2-by-8s spiked together). This header will serve as a base for the 2-by-4s that

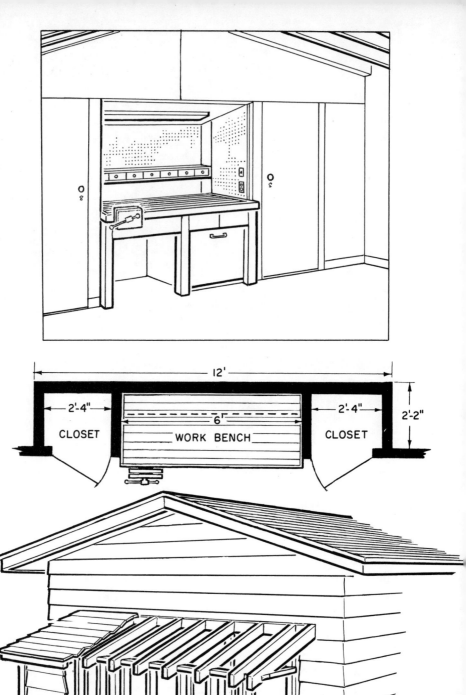

12'

2'-4"

CLOSET

6'

WORK BENCH

2'-4"

CLOSET

2'-2"

go the rest of the way to the roof and also as a nailing base for the 2″-by-4″ rafters of the lean-to. Use triple studs as support at the header ends.

Because the lean-to is light in weight, its foundation can be minimal. It can be a concrete slab poured in a securely staked 2″-by-4″ form over a 6″-deep bed of coarse gravel for drainage. In cases where the garage floor is above grade, it may be necessary to prepare a supporting foundation wall to match that of the existing structure.

In attaching the lean-to, first remove shingles, clapboard or other exterior finish from the existing structure. Do it carefully; you may be able to salvage much of it for use on the new addition. Frame the structure with 2-by-4s on 16″ centers. Notch the 2″-by-4″ rafters where they cross the 2″-by-4″ cap that tops the stud wall. Where the rafters attach to the existing structure, they should rest on a 2″-by-3″ ledger strip nailed to the bottom of the 4″-by-8″ header which bridges the opening. Nail the rafters to the header.

You can enclose the structure with ⅜″ plywood sheathing. Finish sidewalls and roof to match the existing structure. Before applying roofing, flash joints between roof and wall with aluminum or copper sheet to seal out the weather.

Example of an extension lean-to built on the non-bearing wall of a garage to allow for a workbench and closets.

5

Storage: Walls / Shelves

PERFORATED HARDBOARD. The most commonly used system for storing tools is to hang them on walls of perforated hardboard. A variety of special hooks and hanging devices are available that fit in the perforations. For average service, ⅛″ hardboard is satisfactory, but for hanging heavy items like sledges, chain saws, and shelves, ¼″ panels are recommended. Panels are available prefinished in a number of attractive colors.

Most hanging devices are of metal or plastic. Many of the metal hangers require special stabilizers so they won't pull out of the holes every time you unhook a tool. But even with stabilizers, devices tend to pull out of holes. Plastic devices hold fairly well without stabilizers but are apt to break, especially if moved from one set of holes to another.

Don't skimp on hangers. If you don't have the right types, or enough of them, you can't make efficient use of the available storage space. Often, after removing a tool, there may be some doubt as to which hanger it belongs on. For this reason, it is often helpful to label tool locations or to draw outlines of the tools on the storage board.

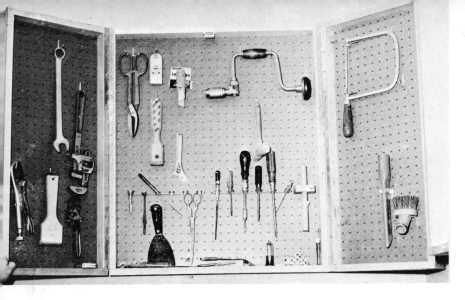

Perforated hardboard is ideal for hanging hand tools over a workbench. Here a hinged cabinet backed with the material keeps a variety of tools within reach but when closed protects them from dust and rust.

This garage was paneled with perforated hardboard, and garden tools and paint supplies neatly stored on hangers and shelves. For heavy tools like these, ¼″ board should be used. Light hand tools can be hung on ⅛″ board.

Special hangers are available for hanging all kinds of items on perforated hardboard. These shelf hangers support heavy paint cans and even lengths of lumber.

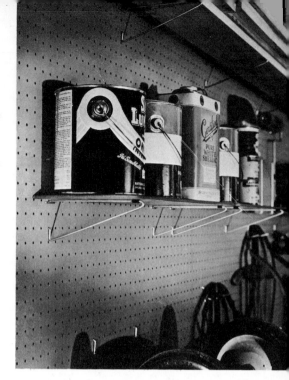

Space that might otherwise be wasted at the end of a workbench can be used for tool storage by installing a panel of perforated hardboard. A door backed with same material doubles the storage area and keeps tools clean.

Here a panel is mounted on the side of a table saw to hang saw blades, tools, and accessories needed in this area.

Holes drilled so close to the edge of a plywood strip that they break through the front make convenient hangers for handled tools on this perforated hardboard storage wall.

Perforated storage panels can go places other than walls. They can line the inside of cabinets, several can be set in a series of slots and individual panels pulled out for tool access, or they can be framed and hinged so they can be opened like the pages of a book. The hinging arrangement makes it possible to hang several layers of tools on one wall space.

When perforated panels are set flat against the wall, they should be offset sufficiently so that hooks can be inserted through the holes.

SOLID STORAGE WALLS.   Walls of ¼″ plywood, or of tongue-and-groove boards, make a superior surface for hanging tools, especially with screw-in devices. Large clothesline hooks can handle big, heavy tools and equipment. Cup hooks can manage smaller items. To hang an electric drill from a cup hook, tighten a screw eye in its chuck.

In this shop, walls of solid board paneling serve as a complete tool storage area. By using a variety of screw-in devices and wooden racks, the shop owner was able to hang his hand tools in a neat and convenient arrangement.

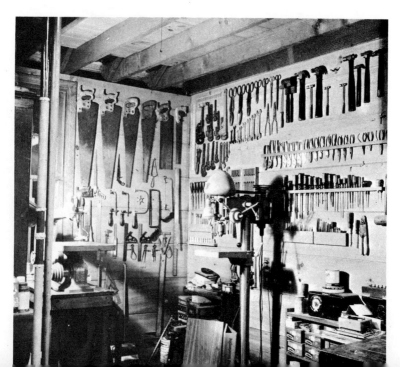

Wooden blocks shaped to fit the handles or frames of saws serve as efficient hanging devices on this storage wall. L-screws and broom clamps are also good hangers.

On a plaster wall, scrap pieces of plywood provide the necessary backing for attaching hanging devices. Broom clamps and dowels on the plywood are used effectively to store handsaws.

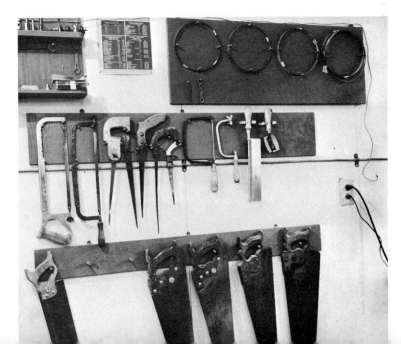

This paneled wall of Ponderosa pine deserved a set of elegant hangers. Strips of $\frac{5}{4}''$ sugar pine were dadoed and doweled to accept hand tools.

Clothesline hooks come as screw-in or plate-and-screw types. Other available hooks include clothes hooks, steel hooks that screw in, utility hangers, and hammock sets (in which hooks are set on a swivel).

As an aid in hanging items, you can get handle holders commonly used for hanging brooms. They can be tapped on with a hammer; some types attach with only adhesive. Swing-out racks and dryers, commonly used in bathrooms and kitchens, are other useful storage devices which are easily attached to a wood wall.

Wood blocks, custom-shaped to fit saws, pliers, snips, scrapers, nail pullers, and a variety of other tools also make highly satisfactory hanging devices on wood walls. Saw hangers should have a turnbuckle arrangment so the saw won't slip off. This is especially important when a saw is mounted on a door.

Old garden hose cut in short pieces and attached vertically is good for small tools like screwdrivers. Cut the hose at an angle and the short lengths are easy to tack up. Use a pair to receive plier handles. For tools too wide to drop through a hose opening, slit the hose down the front.

Attractive hangers that will accommodate many kinds of tools can be made from 2″-by-2″ boards slotted at 1½″ or 2″ intervals. Or similar strips may be drilled to receive screwdrivers, files, pliers, nail sets, etc.

For tools like chisels you can make dado cuts in ¾″-by-2″ board, and mount the board so the cuts are against the wall. Dowels set into backing strips at a slight tilt make excellent holders for hammers, snips, etc.

Most people prefer open tool panels for tools that are in frequent use. In planning such storage, provide not only for tools you now have but for others you will acquire in the future.

A window and its frame were utilized to the full as a tool storage area in this shop.

Space under the eaves that would be wasted in this attic shop is filled with a plywood panel on which tools are hung on broom clamps, dowels, and screw-in hooks. Area behind the panel is also used for storage and is closed off by a door.

Magnetic holders made for cutlery are convenient for keeping light tools like putty knives within easy reach on the side of the workbench.

SHELVES.   For many tools and most supplies, shelves are the answer. Shelves can be hung on walls, can serve as room dividers, and can be installed inside and on top of cabinets and under benches. They can go on the back of closet doors, between studs, or be hung from rafters. Most shelves are hung level, but to display tools like chisels and screwdrivers they can be set at a front-to-back slant.

Pine shelving is the most popular for use in a workshop. It's expensive if you buy top grades, but the price plummets when you get down to #3 grade. It comes as wide as nominal 12″, which is actually about 11½″. This width can be increased slightly by nailing strips on either side. When you do, reinforce the ends of the shelf with a ¾″-by-¾″ strip. Where a shelf

Shelves between two beam-supporting posts in a basement shop store tiers of numbered boxes and glass jars. Contents of boxes are listed in an index according to number.

width much greater than 11½″ is desired, a good solution is to use plywood.

Shelves made of ¾″ stock should not span more than 30″. Heavy tools and supplies will make any shelf longer than that sag. To stiffen a shelf board against sagging, glue and nail a 1½″-wide strip to its front edge.

The simplest support for a shelf is a cleat at each end. A cleat along the rear edge gives added strength and support. Cleats can be of ¾″ half-round molding, 1″-by-2″ boards or equivalent. Ends can also be supported by rests of metal or plastic. These rests push-fit into holes drilled in wood side-supports. By providing a vertical series of holes, you can quickly move a shelf to a new position. Shelf rests may fit into vertical metal standards.

Metal standards can also be used to support brackets for shelves. Brackets come in sizes from 6″ to 14″. Tension-pole standards can be set between floor and ceiling for supporting shelves.

Closely spaced studs grooved to accept ¼″ plywood shelves turn one end of this shop into a complete storage wall for fasteners and hardware.

Cabinet to hold jars for small parts storage has shelves of 1/8″ hardboard supported on quarter-round moldings. Strips across the shelf fronts keep jars from slipping off.

Metal standards with clip supports are available in hardware stores and make shelf installation an easy job.

If a shelf adjoins a window, round off its corner and it won't be an obstruction.

The small parts rack in the shop of Marshall W. Geletee has ten shelves, each with five jars for screws, bolts, etc. When not in use the rack folds up between the floor joists, leaving the area clear.

Brackets which are inserted in the holes of perforated hardboard are another type of shelf support.

For shelves on the back of a door, nail a ledge along the front to keep things from falling off when the door is swung. You can increase the storage capacity of shelves by nailing a wide board ledge across their front and converting them into bins. Such a bin is ideal for keeping wiping rags, plumbing fittings, nails, and miscellaneous tools.

Metal shelving is low in cost and excellent for shop use. It can be bought in knockdown kits, with shelves spaced as you desire. You can buy additional shelves if closer spacing is required. Some steel storage units are available with strong card-

This tool rack was designed to fit the Beginner's Workbench in Chapter 3. The rack can either be fastened to the bench top or hung on the wall over the bench. *Courtesy American Plywood Co.*

Plans for Building the Beginner's Workbench Tool Rack

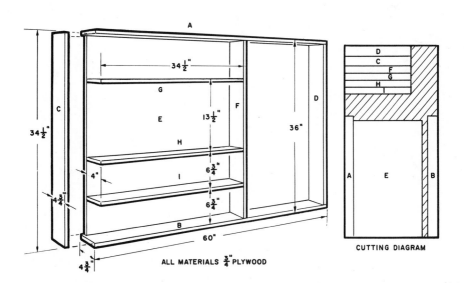

ALL MATERIALS ¾" PLYWOOD

CUTTING DIAGRAM

board boxes, good for many storage uses.

Instead of using boards for shelves between exposed wall studs, you can use rain gutters. They are especially good for a miscellany of screws, nails, nuts, and bolts.

You can get high utilization from shelves by designing them to accommodate jars and boxes. Cigar boxes, peanut-butter jars, cans are only a few of the kinds of containers that may be used. So that you'll know what's in boxes (not easy to remember when you have a hundred or more), give each a number and have an index listing what each number contains.

Circular saw blades can be stored in shelves divided like a record cabinet. A divider should separate each blade.

Shelves for the storage of light bulbs can have holes drilled in them to accept the bulb screw-base. Along the shelf edge, place a label to clearly identify bulb type and size.

When making shelves that are fastened permanently to side supports, the preferred technique is to make a dado or groove in each side. When the shelf is inserted in the dado, fasten it there with glue, and screws or nails. As an added touch, if you don't want the dado to show, make it a "stopped dado," ending it just short of the front face of the upright support.

6 | Storage: Cabinets / Chests

Workshop cabinets and chests should be simple and rugged, but they can also be attractive. Avoid the urge to plunge in and build a single cabinet or chest before you decide what the whole shop is going to be like. First establish an overall plan; otherwise you'll end with a mishmash. A makeshift shop won't be pleasant or relaxing to work in. It is just as easy to create a shop with a degree of uniformity.

Restrict yourself in the use of materials. Try to keep storage units similar in appearance. If your cabinets have flush doors, don't put lipped fronts on the drawers, and try to use matching hardware throughout.

Perhaps you have old kitchen cabinets, secondhand desks, shabby bookcases—all of which would be handy to use in the shop. If some are tall, others short, some narrow and some deep, overcome these discrepancies by cutting the big ones down to desired size and building the little ones up. Differences can be deemphasized by application of unifying features. Base cabinets can be unified by giving them all a common, continuous top. Drawers that don't match can be unified by painting them all the same color and giving them matching hardware. If nothing else, line up the tops of doors and drawers. If a piece is beyond remedy, you can still salvage its parts.

Whether you are building new storage units, or readapting old ones, plan your design to serve specific needs. Measure shelves and divide drawers to accommodate specific tools and supplies. Plan their locations so these tools and supplies are near their point of most frequent use. Avoid "general storage." Plan storage for portable power tools, plumbing tools and supplies, for concrete and masonry tools and supplies, for electrical/electronic tools and supplies, for painting equipment and supplies, etc.

Open shelves are the easiest to build, but doors offer protection against dust and rust, hide clutter, and can give security against unauthorized use. If you build shelf units, it's usually easy enough to add doors later.

BUILDING THE BOX.   A storage unit is essentially a box. In this box you place shelves or drawers. The box can be any shape. It can rest on its own bottom, or on legs or a base.

The materials you use for building storage units will be mostly ¾″ fir plywood or 1″-by-12″ shelving boards. For economy, the plywood will be interior grade, good one side (G1S); the shelving will be #3.

The advantage of plywood is that it offers widths up to 4′ without the necessity of piecing. The disadvantages are that

A cabinet or chest is basically a box in which shelves or drawers are installed. It can be assembled with butt joints or, as shown here, with a rabbet joint at the top and a dado joint at the bottom. Be sure to use glue with nails or screws on all joints.

Plywood is the ideal cabinet material because it comes in panel sizes, but this craftsman decided to save money by using #3 pine shelving. Two 1-by-12s joined with white glue and corrugated fasteners make a wide panel.

To protect the interior against dampness and make cleanup easier, the base of the cabinet is off the floor. It fits in dadoes cut in the sides.

Hardboard back gives a cabinet rigidity and seals out dust. It can be nailed directly to the edges of the case, or set in a rabbet ½″ wide and ¼″ deep for a neater finish.

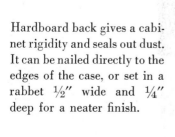
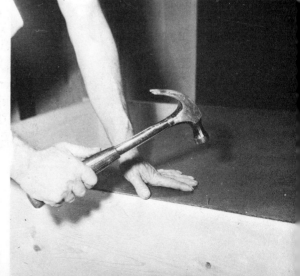

it is a little harder to assemble (because of the problem of edge nailing), it shows edge grain that is unsightly, and it may delaminate in areas subject to excessive moisture.

The advantage of boards is that they are easier to handle, join, and paint. The disadvantages are that usually they don't come wider than 11½", they have a tendency to warp and twist, and they aren't as strong as plywood.

Tempered hardboard has a place, too. Because of its smooth surface, it makes unexcelled drawer bottoms. Because of its panel size and economy, it makes excellent cabinet backs. You'll want cabinet backs. They add rigidity and seal against dust, moisture, and small animals.

You can cover base cabinets with a top to provide a working surface. Typical stand-up height would then be 32", sitdown height 28". Depth (distance from front to back) can be 18" to 30". If a hanging cabinet is to go above it, the clearance between the two would be about 15".

If cabinets run from floor to ceiling, plan upper shelves for dead storage or seldom-used items. You can't see into a drawer whose top is more than chin high, so plan accordingly.

Once the case has been constructed, the interior can be divided according to your needs. Cleats can be used to support shelves or drawers.

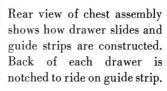

Rear view of chest assembly shows how drawer slides and guide strips are constructed. Back of each drawer is notched to ride on guide strip.

Cabinets may be built as free-standing units or, as here, built-ins. Proper use of a level may spell the difference between success and failure. Keep *construction* level and plumb, disregarding slope of walls and floor.

To make a cabinet turn a corner, miter the shelves with glue and corrugated fasteners. This joint is stronger than a butt joint.

WOODWORKING JOINTS.   There are all kinds of joints, but only a few have significant application in constructing shop furnishings. Strength and rigidity are the prime consider-ations. The butt joint and the dado joint can handle almost everything. Occasionally you can use a half-lap, spline, and lock mortise.

Regardless of whether the top of a cabinet overhangs its ends and front or fits flush, it can be attached with a simple butt joint. If it overhangs, you gain a little something by making it a dado joint.

Simple dado cuts in the sides of a cabinet offer the best joint support for a shelf. If you use a butt joint for shelves, you can gain strength by resting the shelf on a wood strip. A cabinet back can be applied flush, but you'll gain in rigidity by recess-ing it in a rabbet. Secure all joints, wherever they are, with white glue *and* nails or screws. In most cases, use 2″ finishing nails or 1¼″ #8 flat-head wood screws.

Cabinets can be supported on legs, which you buy and attach with screws, or on a base. A simple sturdy base is a 2-by-4 running along the back, with other 2-by-4s recessed 2½″ for toe space at front and sides. The cabinet bottom is nailed or screwed to this frame. Cabinet sides also can run to the floor, being notched at the front to receive the toe-space board.

HOW TO BUILD DRAWERS.   If a cabinet is a box, a drawer is merely a sliding box. A workshop needs numerous drawers, so you ought to know how to build them.

A drawer front may be inset flush with the frame, or it may have a lip. The inset drawer is easier to build, but is much harder to fit. A drawer needs ⅟₁₆″ clearance. A lip hides this gap so that clearance differences aren't apparent.

The biggest strain on a drawer is at its front joints. Yank-ing on a drawer tends to pull its front loose from its sides. Most commercial drawers have dovetail joints at their front, and if you have a router and a dovetailing kit, this is a good chance to enjoy the pleasure of making these joints.

The easiest drawer-front joint to make is a simple butt joint with the drawer sides overlapping both front and back. For appearance and added security, a facing of ¼″ plywood is applied over the front, or ½″ plywood if the facing extends to make a lip.

You can substitute dowels for dovetail joints on drawer fronts. First, apply glue to the joint and tack the parts together with a couple of nails. Then drill holes the size of the dowel to a depth of at least three times the thickness of the drawer's sides. Apply glue to the dowels and drive them into place. Use grooved dowels. If you use smooth dowel stock, flatten one side by sanding, or cut a groove on it and taper the dowel-end slightly. If you don't flatten the side or cut a groove, excess glue or trapped air can't escape and the dowel won't fill the hole properly.

A third type of joint can be made by cutting dadoes in the drawer front into which the sides are fitted and angled nailed and glued.

The backboard of a drawer should be recessed in a dado cut in each side to a depth that is half the thickness of the side. The dado should be ½″ to ¾″ from the rear edge. If you don't have the tools or know-how to make a dado joint, a butt joint here will suffice.

One way to attach the drawer bottom is to groove the inner face of the front and sides (but not the back). The drawer back is not cut as deep as the sides. Its bottom edge is flush with the tops of the grooves cut in the sides. This makes it possible to slide the drawer bottom into place under it.

A drawer bottom can be ⅛″ or ¼″ tempered hardboard or ¼″ plywood. The groove into which it fits should be cut at least ¼″ up from the bottom of the sides and should be a shade wider than its thickness. The groove's depth should be a shade less than half the thickness of the side. Plane the edges of the bottom panel slightly if the fit is too tight. The bottom will extend over the drawer back and should be attached to it with small nails. The bottom is not glued anywhere.

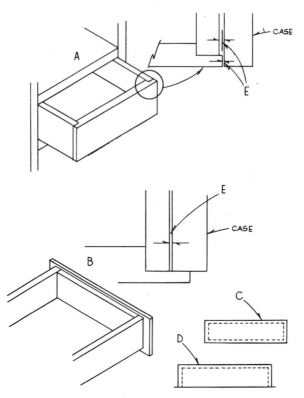

Drawer front can fit flush with the case edges (A) or over-hang the edges (B). Rabbet joints are used in both instances. If the sides are simply butted against the front, and a front panel applied, the overlap can be on four edges (C) or three (D). Provide clearance of $\frac{1}{16}''$ (E) so drawer works smoothly.

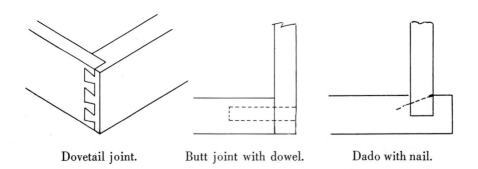

Dovetail joint.   Butt joint with dowel.   Dado with nail.

The ½" sides of this drawer are attached to the ¾" front by recessing them in dadoes. Glue, and finishing nails driven from the side at an angle, provide satisfactory holding power.

The sides and back of this drawer, or tray, are higher than the front, making the contents easily accessible. It's all built with butt joints. Note groove along the side. The tray will slide on angled supports which will be inserted into this groove.

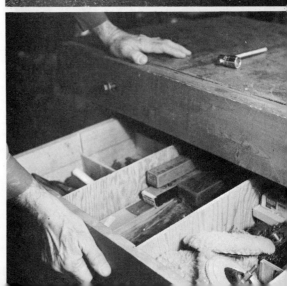

Dividing a drawer helps to keep it neat and provides sections for different types of equipment. Slots for the partitions should be cut before the drawer is assembled.

If slots have not been cut in the drawer before assembly, an insert arrangement can be made of $\frac{1}{2}''$ stock without losing much storage space.

When dividers cross each other, use a half-lap joint to fit the pieces together.

Here is a completely divided drawer. The small tray slides on top of the lower divided section, providing access.

Drawer rests and slides on this divider frame. Middle member of the frame is a guide to keep drawer straight and prevent jamming. The bottom edge of the drawer back is notched to fit the guide, as shown in a previous photo on page 95.

When drawers are big, and will be required to bear heavy loads, manufactured slides are· recommended to insure satisfactory operation. One part of the slide is attached to the side of the chest and the other to drawer (below).

If you don't have a power tool for cutting grooves, you can nail and glue the drawer bottom directly to the edges of the sides, front, and back. In this case, you don't have to cut the drawer back shorter than the sides. To enable the drawer to move easily, nail two ⅛″ strips to the bottom, one on each side.

It is difficult to maintain an orderly drawer unless it is partitioned. Nor will it accommodate as much. Deep drawers can be partitioned to provide two storage levels, with a sliding tray as the upper level. If a drawer is to be divided, dividers may be made of hardboard, plywood, or ½″ solid stock. They are inserted into dadoes cut in the drawer sides. Plan for dividers before you build the drawer. You can't readily cut dadoes after it is assembled. To make dividers for an existing drawer, make a complete slip-in unit of ½″ stock.

A drawer moves on a divider frame, or on slides, and is kept straight by strips called guides. A drawer doesn't rest on the guide but on the frame or slides, which should be lubricated with soap or melted paraffin for easier action. Since shop drawers are usually heavily laden, for easiest operation attach ball-bearing slides.

For economy, you can attach runners to the drawer sides and cut grooves in the case sides. The alternative is to cut the

Technique for handling heavy bottom drawers is to put them on casters. Drawer bottom will be a loose, removable panel.

Here is completed tray (shown in previous photo) resting on its slides. By attaching each pair of slides only after the drawer below is installed, proper fit and clearances are assured.

grooves in the drawer sides and attach supporting strips to the case sides. The latter is a technique for adding a drawer to an existing case. Instead of wood strips, you can use aluminum angle as supports.

When there is no means of side support, as when you wish to hang a drawer under a counter or bench top, you can use an aluminum channel attached to the top. Drill screw holes through both sides of the channel and you won't have difficulty making the attachment. Or you can cut an L-shaped hanger from $\frac{3}{4}''$ stock. Easier still, make the L out of two separate pieces.

Good small drawers for small parts can have sheet-metal bottoms. Let the side edges of the bottom project so they can slide in saw-kerf slots cut into a box frame.

Once you know the principles, you can make such improvisations as a chest in which the drawers are all cigar boxes.

CABINET DOORS. The two basic kinds of shop doors are those that slide and those that swing. Sliding doors are easier to install, but they provide access to only half a cabinet at a time. You can buy sliding-door tracks of wood, metal, or plastic for $\frac{1}{8}''$, $\frac{1}{4}''$, or larger panels. Panels may be of hardboard, plywood, plastic, or glass. The top track has deeper grooves than the lower one, and panels are inserted by lifting them into the upper grooves and then dropping them into the lower ones.

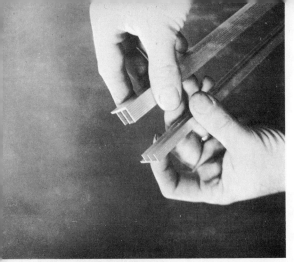

Sliding door tracks, whether of aluminum, plastic, or wood, come in pairs. The upper track has deeper grooves to permit inserting and removing the panel.

Wood track can be quickly installed in a cabinet with finishing nails, whereas metal track requires screws. Finishing wood track to match the cabinet presents fewer problems than with metal.

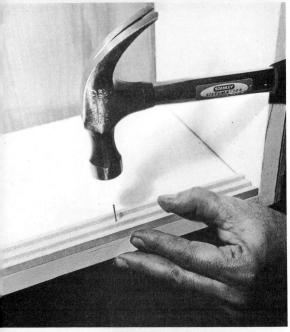

To mark a sliding panel for size, raise it all the way into the upper track, then mark for cutting even with the top of the bottom track.

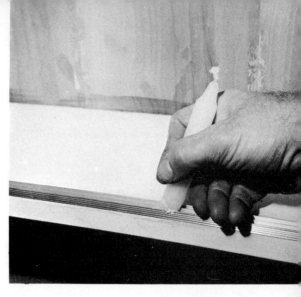

Lubricating track with paraffin eases operation of sliding panel. Secret of building smooth-working doors is to have perfectly square panels and parallel tracks.

You can rip your own track out of wood strips, cut integral grooves into the frame of your cabinet, or create grooves with surface-mounted wood strips.

A popular type of pull for sliding panels is a shallow cup which fits into a hole drilled in the door. For convenience, insert a pull of this kind at the end of each panel.

If you have a shelf unit that you want to put behind sliding panels, it may be necessary to extend the top, bottom, and sides so they extend forward of the shelves and allow clearance for the sliding panels.

The simplest swing doors for shop cabinets are ones that overlap the front edges of the case. They are preferably hung with pin hinges, but you can use butt hinges.

Swing doors may be inset within a case. These are harder to fit than overlapping doors, but some people prefer their style. These can be hung with mortised butt hinges, surface hinges, hinges with an exposed barrel, or semiconcealed hinges. You can get no-mortise butt hinges and save yourself some work. Continuous-style hinges give superior support to recessed doors and have a distinctively handsome appearance.

A third type of swing door for shop cabinets is lipped. The lip may partially overlap the opening, or may completely cover the front edges of the case. There are several types of semiconcealed hinges for lipped doors.

Though some hinges are "self-closing" and stay shut without a catch, in most cases you will need some type of catch to

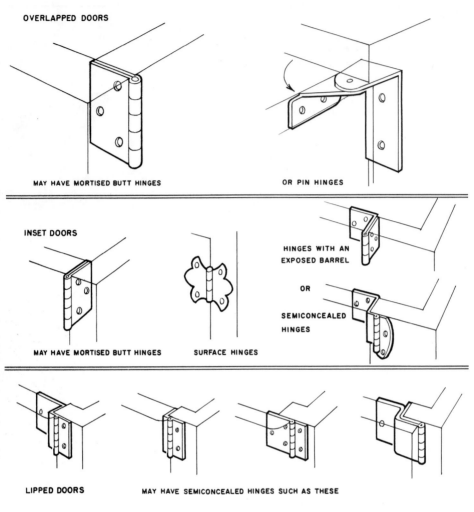

OVERLAPPED DOORS

MAY HAVE MORTISED BUTT HINGES

OR PIN HINGES

INSET DOORS

HINGES WITH AN EXPOSED BARREL

OR

SEMICONCEALED HINGES

MAY HAVE MORTISED BUTT HINGES

SURFACE HINGES

LIPPED DOORS

MAY HAVE SEMICONCEALED HINGES SUCH AS THESE

Methods of hinging overlapped, inset, and lipped doors.

keep doors closed. Two simple types are magnetic and double-roller friction catches. If you want to lock the doors, get a cupboard lock.

Single doors require a stop so they won't swing inward. A cleat does the job. If a cabinet has double doors, it needs a center-stile stop. For flush, inset doors the stile requires a cleat along each edge to act as a stop. Or the stile and door edges can be rabbeted so they form a half-lap joint where they meet.

Pin hinges are almost invisible on overlapped doors. Top of door must be mortised slightly to receive this style of hinge.

When pin hinges are attached to the side of a door, one half must be recessed in a slot.

STORAGE-BENCH COMBO. Accompanying drawings show a complete workshop that grows on a modular plan. All units are based on the construction details for the Lock-up Workbench in Chapter 3. First, you build unit A. It provides storage, lighting, and a working surface at which you can stand or sit. Next, you can build B. It provides additional storage as well as more working surface. Units C and D provide a variety of other kinds of storage. All units are coordinated and combine to create an harmonious shop environment.

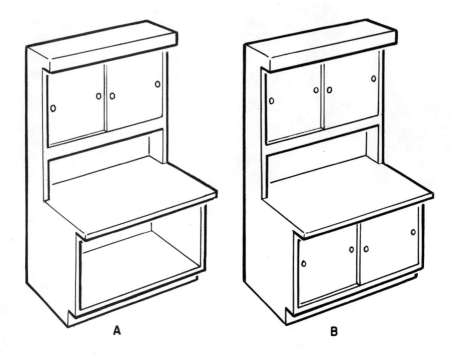

A   B

Complete workshop grows with modular units that provide bench and storage space. Construction details are the same as for Lock-up Workbench in Chapter 3 except that units are built half the size.

For economy, you can build the units of fir plywood. Birch is better looking and more durable, but costs considerably more. You may find it worth the difference.

You can make the work surface 30″, 32″, or 34″ high, which ever best suits your size and work habits. You can install sliding or swinging doors on the base cabinet of unit A, or leave it open to provide storage for lumber shorts, folding sawhorses, or a toolbox.

CONSTRUCTION TIPS

• If, instead of making freestanding storage units, you're making built-ins, use your level religiously. Don't forget that your floors may slope and your walls may be out of plumb. A

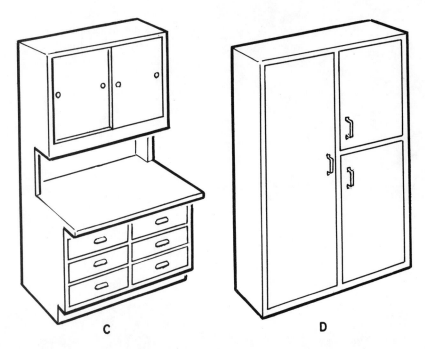

C   D

level is insurance that you'll get true horizontals and verticals. If you build out of plumb, shelves will slant, drawers may roll open, and doors refuse to fit. Use shims wherever needed to make your structure level. Wood shingles, because of their wedge shape, make especially good shim material. Use a pencil compass to transfer the irregularities of a wall to a board or panel that is being butt-fitted against it.

• If you are working with plywood, carefully lay out parts needed on each panel to minimize waste and confirm that your grain directions are right.

• If you have swing room, hinge doors give maximum accessibility. Don't overlook the possibility of using bottom-hinged cabinet doors and special drop-leaf supports. They can provide extra working space.

• If you want to reinforce a butt joint, you can do it easily with dowels and glue. It doesn't matter if dowel ends show.

• Dowels are also a good way to overcome the lack of holding power in the end-grain of plywood. Insert with glue a

Some storage devices are so good and inexpensive that it pays to buy rather than to build them. Plastic drawer case shown here is one example. It is ideal for storing small parts.

Everything displayed on the floor is stored in this cabinet, which is mounted on casters and also serves as an outboard support for sawing long pieces of lumber. This illustrates how orderly storage can reduce clutter.

⅜" dowel about ⅜" back, and parallel to, the end of the end-grain piece. Pre-drill holes through the end-grain and into the dowel before driving screws.

    • Miter joints aren't any stronger than ordinary butt joints, but it's easy to give them added strength. Cut 45-degree saw kerfs into edges of meeting pieces and set thin spline strips into the grooves.

    • Instead of nailing through sides into shelves, toenail from underneath shelves into sides. In that way you avoid marring the sides of your cabinet with overzealous hammer blows or with holes you have to fill.

7

Power and Light

Few shops start out with enough power or adequate lighting. There are seldom enough outlets, or outlets in the right places. Lighting is makeshift rather than planned. To improve the situation in your workshop it may be necessary to do an elaborate job of rewiring, but you may be able to get by with only a few improvements requiring little skill and a minimum of equipment.

SIMPLE IMPROVEMENTS.   One of the easiest improvements to make in your shop is to replace existing two-prong outlets with grounded three-prong outlets. This eliminates the nuisance of having to use an adapter to fit power tools to two-prong sockets.

Another practical improvement is to replace single outlets with duplex ones. It's just a matter of substituting a new device and plate. Then you won't have to unplug a lamp when you want to plug in a drill.

A circuit is a power line that originates at the service center (fuse or circuit-breaker box). A minimum of two, preferably three circuits is required for a shop. If you now have a single circuit supplying both lighting fixtures and outlets,

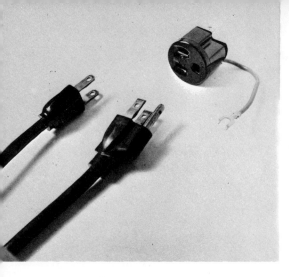

Most power tools have three-pronged plugs like the one at right. The adapter in front of it allows you to plug into a standard socket and ground the tool by fastening the end of the grounding wire, which is U-shaped, under a screw in the outlet faceplate.

adding a second circuit will enable you to keep light and power needs separate. This means you won't be left in the dark when one of your power tools blows a fuse or trips a circuit breaker, nor will your lights dim when you start up a motor.

A typical lighting circuit is designed to handle 15 amperes and is wired with No. 14 cable. A power circuit should be able to handle 20 amperes and be wired with No. 12 cable.

Installing some type of circuit-breaker system is a good way to guard against blown fuses. Circuit-breaker plugs are available that fit into three-pronged outlets. If an overload occurs, a button in the plug pops up and the tool is automatically disconnected. You can gain this same convenience by substituting screw-in circuit breakers for fuses in your fuse box. You can also ease the nuisance of blown fuses by installing a special fuse box within the shop to protect one or more branch circuits.

Adding plug-in facilities in your shop without actually adding new outlets is fairly simple. One method is to use an extension box, generally a 4"-by-4" metal box wired with two duplex receptacles and covered by a plate. An extension cord connects it to an outlet. This gives four plug-in places instead of one. If desired, it can be combined with a switch controlling each duplex receptacle.

Another way is to mount a "power pack" on your stationary tool. It may include two three-prong outlets, an on-off toggle switch, and a safety light to indicate when power is on. Power packs are commercially available.

To bring more power into the shop, run a single 40- or 50-amp cable from the service entry to a sub-box.

Installing a master switch in a closet or other hidden place enables you to shut off all shop circuits with a single flick—a particularly good idea when small children are apt to enter the shop.

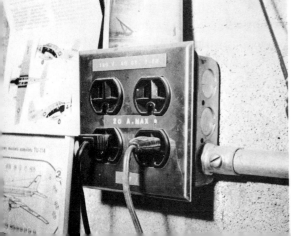

Label power outlets clearly to be sure which circuit you are using and how much current it can supply.

If you have more than one circuit in the shop, you'll find it convenient to tag each outlet, so you know immediately which circuit it's on and which fuse controls it. The tag can also include data as to amps, voltage, cycles, etc.

Often service centers have one or more circuits that are not in use. In a circuit-breaker setup, you may be able to gain extra circuits by installing duplex breakers. If you have no spare circuits, and your house power is already inadequate, you may want to consider installing a new, larger service.

MORE POWER FOR YOUR SHOP.   A few years ago, a 60-ampere service was considered standard. Now, many homeowners are finding even 100-ampere service inadequate. With a dishwasher, drier, air conditioner, water heater, range, even the furnace and boiler being powered by electricity, more and more people are turning to 200-ampere service.

Power pack can be mounted on power-tool stand, provides extra outlets and an on-off switch. It has a light that glows to show if power is on.

Plug at left has its own built-in circuit breaker. Mini-Breaker, center, can replace an ordinary fuse like one at right and cut off power when overload occurs.

Installing a new service does not necessarily mean tearing out the old. For example, if you were to install a new 200-ampere entry, a 100-ampere breaker could be included in it and from it a cable run to "feed" the existing service. If you wish, the new service can be in a new location. There need be no disruption while the new service is being wired. The power company will run in new, heavier lines from the pole, but you may have to provide a new meter socket and cable from it to the service center box.

The cost of converting from 60 to 100 amps isn't cheap, but in many areas, the power company will finance the job and charge monthly payments for a year or two on your regular electric bill.

Here's how to calculate how much power you need for your shop. A typical ½ hp motor draws 7 amps. Good practice requires that it be on a 20-amp circuit.

If you have ample current, provide a separate 20-amp circuit for every major stationary power tool. If you have, or plan to acquire, an arc welder, even the smallest requires a 30- or 40-amp circuit.

A 100-watt bulb draws 1 amp. If you are hard-pressed for power, substitute fluorescent tubes. They will give 2 to 4 times as much light for the same current.

If you have circuits without much on them, you can gain convenience by adding new outlets. At the workbench, one of the best arrangements is the use of Electrostrips. These are power-carrying strips into which you can snap receptacles at any point. Electrostrips can take off from an outlet box or a cable end. The strip can be nailed or screwed to any convenient surface.

If you have the money to spend, the best system of all is a "lighting duct." This is a kind of power system used in industry. It is an overhead track, about 1″ square in cross section, into which a variety of plugs, trolleys, or light fixtures can be connected. The duct can be mounted flush to the ceiling or suspended. The duct can be arranged in any pattern on the

Electrostrip along front edge of bench or on wall behind it brings power wherever it is needed. The strip can be connected to an outlet box or cable end.

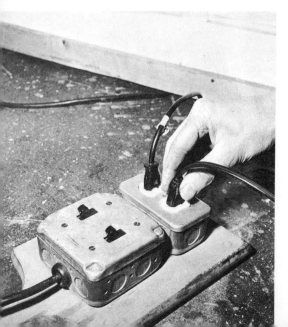

Duplex outlet with switches and extension cord can be mounted on a breadboard to make a mobile plug-in platform for power tools.

Outlet on the side of the house is convenient for outside jobs requiring power tools. Snap-up covers protect against dirt and rain. Make sure outlet is grounded.

When adding extra outlets, you can sometimes avoid difficulties in snaking cable through walls by installing outlets in the floor. Special types are available for the purpose.

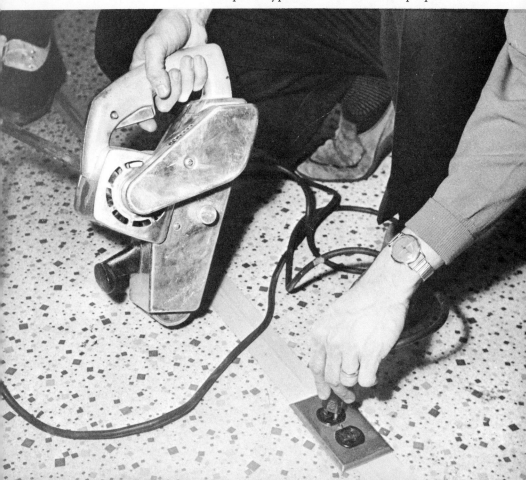

ceiling so that power is available anywhere in the shop. Power tools can be connected by drop lines in the center of the floor, eliminating hazardous trailing wires.

DOING YOUR OWN WIRING.   Most local codes permit the homeowner to do his own wiring, provided he has a permit. Your wiring will then be inspected for conformance to regulations. Often, an electrical inspector will offer you good advice on how your wiring may best be done. There are usually very sound reasons for every code requirement, even though it may not readily be apparent to the nonprofessional. Faulty wiring is a major cause of fire in the home. You may only be cheating yourself if you try to get away with a wiring violation.

Even though the existing wiring in your house may lack a grounding wire, it must be included with all new work. All new outlets must be grounded. Following is a list of do's and don'ts to bear in mind when undertaking a wiring job.

1. Be sure to insert a fiber or plastic bushing to protect wire from the cut end on BX cable.

2. Never bury a box. If you no longer have use for a box at its present location, don't cover it with plasterboard. If you can't convert it to an outlet, switch, or light, cover it with a blank plate.

If you add partitions when creating your shop, you automatically provide a good place for running electric cable. Outlet box with its own mounting strap is easily attached to a stud.

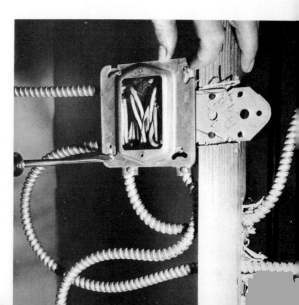

3. *Don't crowd boxes with wiring. The typical outlet or switch box should have no more than one cable leading in and one leading out. Use a 4"-by-4" box when more than this must be accommodated.*

4. *Don't cut wire leads short. Allow enough length so that a switch or outlet can be pulled completely free of the box when it is connected.*

5. *Don't connect more than one wire under a switch or outlet screw. If more than one wire is to be connected to a screw terminal, connect a single wire to the terminal and then join this wire to the other wires by means of a solderless connector.*

6. *Never work on a box when it is live. Shut off the power. Don't assume that all wiring in a single box is from the same circuit. If you're in doubt about current being off, check terminals or wires with a test lamp before you touch them.*

7. *Don't mount fluorescent fixtures on combustible surfaces. The ballast inside can get hot enough to start a fire. Use metal brackets to allow an air space between the fixture and the surface. In some cases, mounting the fixture on asbestos board over wood is permissible.*

8. *Use no more than 80 percent of a circuit capacity. On a 15-amp, 115-volt circuit you have 1380 watts, not 1725 watts.*

Outlets for ceiling fixtures and ventilators are mounted on a support between joists. Box can be positioned anywhere along the support.

9. Always connect black wires to brass terminals, white wires to chrome terminals. Except in switch wiring, always connect black to black, white to white, red to red.

GOOD LIGHTING.   There are three important reasons for having good lighting. First, and most important, is safety. When you can't really see what you are doing, you're inviting trouble. Second, is efficiency. It's easy enough to make errors in measuring, marking, and cutting even when the light is good. When you have to strain to see, you'll make more errors and you'll waste energy. Third, good lighting is more pleasant. A dingy shop is depressing, dull, uninspiring. Good lighting is stimulating and invigorating. You feel like working and enjoy it more.

Every ten years in this century business and industry have been doubling lighting levels in office, factory, shop. Brighter lighting does not mean glare. Outdoors, in the shade, it's ten times as bright as you would ever have it in your shop, yet there is no glare. Glare comes when there is excessive contrast between light and dark.

To avoid glare, no part of your shop should be more than three times as brightly lighted as any other part. To accomplish this uniformity of illumination, you first must have supple-

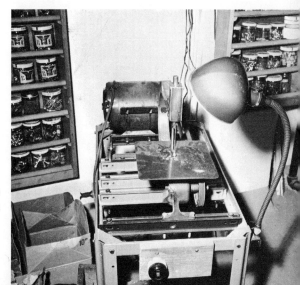

Gooseneck lamp attached to jigsaw stand focuses light on work area.

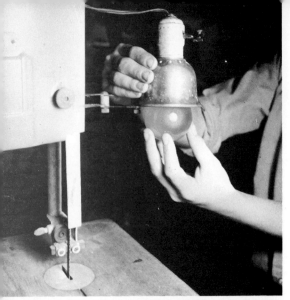

Band saw requires its own light, which can be swung aside when not in use.

Fluorescent desk lamp is adapted to wall use for lighting a specific area where much close work is done.

Never use bare bulbs in a shop. Reflectors are available that screw on the threaded end of socket adapters.

Industrial fluorescent light with its own reflector is first rate for shop use. It can be hung by a chain from an outlet box.

mentary lighting at power tools and at the workbench.

Don't worry about getting your shop too bright. What you do have to avoid is a few bright spots of light. Spread the light around with many low-intensity sources of illumination. Incandescent bulbs are good for spot illumination, such as at a band saw, because they pinpoint light. Fluorescent bulbs are good for general illumination because they spread light.

An industrial fluorescent fixture with two 40-watt lamps, approximately 48″ above the surface, gives good general illumination to a workbench area, but for close or precision work you will have to supplement it with another fixture. Gooseneck lamps are good. So are the clamp-on reflector lamps used by photographers.

Never use a bare bulb. Put a good reflector on it, and it will provide nearly twice as much light. The reflector will also spread light more effectively.

Lighting experts measure the level of illumination in footcandles. Theoretically, one footcandle is the amount of light one candle gives at one foot. An incident-light photographic meter can be used to measure footcandles. The noonday sun provides about 10,000 footcandles. General illumination in the home is typically about 10 footcandles, though kitchen or bathroom may be about 30. Benchwork requires a minimum of 70, with close work 100 to 200 or more. Remember, these are minimum standards. The best lighting is natural sunlight, and to match it in a woodworking shop, you would need about 1500 footcandles.

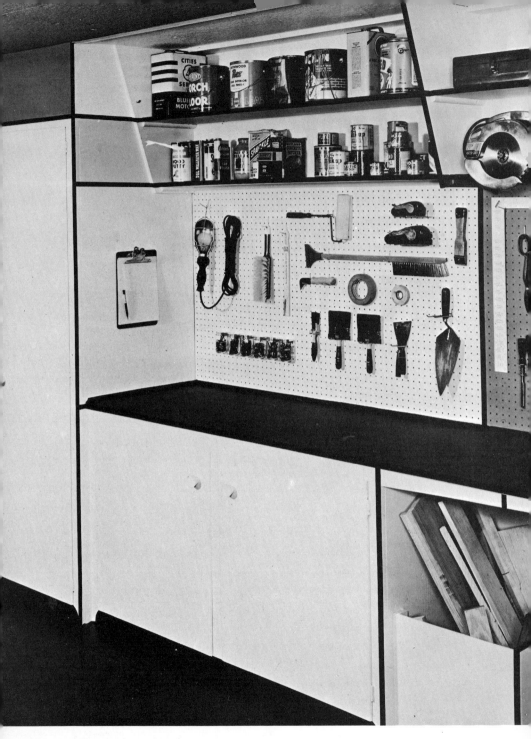

Painting tools and supplies are kept together in this shop corner. Base cabinet provides storage for belt and orbital sanders, sandpaper, paint sprayer, and a bin for rags.

8

The Paint Center

The tools and equipment for painting and paperhanging, for refinishing furniture, for the upkeep and repair of windows, floors, and walls—all these belong in one department. Call it the paint center, because painting and refinishing are the most important part of it, but it logically includes many subsidiary activities. The laying of resilient floor tile and the application of ceramic tile are part of it. So is the application and maintenance of plastic laminates. It is a good place to store all kinds of adhesives, though they might alternately go in the section for nails, screws, and other fastening devices.

The paint center is really not one area, but two. One is the shop section in which you store all the tools and equipment, and perhaps carry on finishing activities. The other is where you store paints, thinners, removers, etc. These materials need not necessarily be kept in the shop.

PAINT STORAGE.   There are definite advantages in storing paints, solvents, and all flammable materials outdoors. The only concern need be for freezing—in the case of latex paints. But even these may include an antifreeze. Read the label for temperature requirements and be guided accordingly. Avoid

125

Tools and adhesives only are stored in this paint center. Paint is kept in an outdoor cabinet. Slanting shelf holds small items within sight and reach. Many supplies are hung in their packages for quick identification.

storing paint supplies near heat or in confined cabinets the sun may turn into hot boxes. The cooler paint is kept, the better.

If you do keep paint and related supplies in the shop, store them on open shelves or in ventilated cabinets. Ventilate paint cabinets by using preforated hardboard as door panels or back panels, or by drilling holes.

Best storage is one-can deep and one-can high. Then you never have to move anything to get at anything else. You can have one or more shelves just high enough for pint cans, but be sure to have at least one shelf high enough for rectangular-shaped gallon cans of thinner, remover, and wood preservative. These cans are 10½″ high; a shelf to accommodate them should be 12″ high. Regular round gallon cans of paint are 8″ high, require a shelf 10″ high. Pint cans are 4″ high, require a 6″ shelf. The space between studs in a wall framed with 2-by-4s is deep enough to store aerosol cans, and you will undoubtedly acquire countless numbers of these.

Your paint dealer will write the color formula of specially color-matched paint right on the can. Add your own information on where in the house the paint was used. Then you won't have to waste time opening cans when you need matching paint for touchups. Don't worry about getting a few splashes or drips

Paints can be stored in a shallow, lockable cabinet mounted on an outside house or garage wall. Temperature requirements on cans of latex paint indicate whether they can be left out in the winter.

Space between wall studs is usually deep enough to accommodate narrow shelves holding paint supplies. Plywood doors should be drilled with ventilation holes.

of paint on the outside of the can. It helps in identification. Paint a patch of the paint on the label to improve the surface for writing.

Paint cans must be tightly closed to prevent deterioration in storage. Cover the can lid with a rag so you won't get splashed by groove paint, and hammer the lid on. After the hammering, turn the can upside down briefly to form an airtight seal.

BRUSHES AND ROLLERS.   Brushes can be stored by hanging them on nails, or keeping them in a drawer if they are first wrapped in brown paper or aluminum foil to maintain their shape. Never rest a brush on its bristles in a paint can.

Paint and brush storage center has an adjustable shelf and ¼″ dowels for holding brushes. Mounted on casters, it rolls out from under the workbench.

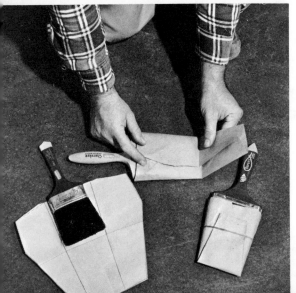

Underside of basement stairs is a handy place to hang paintbrushes on nails (above). If brushes are kept in a drawer, they should be combed and wrapped in brown paper or foil to maintain their shape (left).

Never immerse the brush bristles more than halfway in the paint. A brush can be suspended in a can of solvent by running a wire spindle through a hole drilled in its handle.

The best practice is to buy a good brush and take care of it. A cheap brush won't hold a full load of paint. The paint will run back over the handle onto your hand. Its bristles will shed, and paint won't flow smoothly from it. A good brush is not expensive if it lasts ten years or more.

What is a good brush? Most brushes are "natural bristle" or nylon. In a moderate price range, you'll do better with nylon. Good natural-bristle brushes, made of 100 percent Chinese or Siberian hog bristle, are rare and expensive. If a brush is only partly hog and mostly horsehair or other inferior material, don't buy it. Nylon bristle is best for latex paint. It doesn't absorb water and lose its shape. Natural bristle is superior only for oil paints, enamels, and varnishes.

But all nylon bristle isn't alike. Examine the nylon bristles of a good brush and you'll see that each is tapered so it comes to a fine point. These tapered filaments are the reason the paint flows so well. Cheaper brushes will have only some tapered bristles. In addition, a good brush will have a high proportion of "flagged" or split-ended bristles. These increase its paint holding and smooth-spreading qualities. Poor-quality brushes have blunt-ended filaments.

Run a wire through holes drilled in brush handles to keep bristles from touching bottom when they are being soaked in solvent.

You can also judge a good brush by the quantity of its bristles. Grasp the brush bristles in one hand and you can feel the thickness. Spread the bristles apart and look in the center and you can see just how much is bristle and how much is deception. Look at the brush tip. It should not be blunt across the end, but taper to a point.

Here are some of the brushes you'll probably want in your collection: For large, flat surfaces—a 4″ brush. For trim—a 2″ or 2½″ brush. For furniture, toys, etc.—a varnish or enameling brush 1″ to 3″ wide. A dusting brush is a good investment. So are throwaway brushes, often made of foam, for minor jobs that don't warrant the nuisance of cleaning a brush.

A good part of your painting may be done with rollers. These have different sleeves or covers, depending on whether they are to be used for smooth surfaces, rough surfaces, indoors, outdoors, with latex or oil paint. The most popular sizes have sleeves that are 7″ or 9″ wide, but you can get them 12″, 14″, even 18″. If you're painting a big surface, like a double-garage floor, you'll find a bigger roller a time-saver. You'll also want one with a long handle. Whatever the width of the roller, you need a pan and metal grid to accommodate it, though on a floor you can merely pour a pool of paint and then spread it.

Keep a supply of aluminum foil handy for wrapping brushes when you want to interrupt painting from one day to the next without cleaning them. It's also a good liner for pans. But be sure to remove the foil once the job is done. If you leave it on, drying paint may make it stick. You can also use brown paper as a pan liner. Only the oil will penetrate it.

You will need one or more 9′-by-12′ drop cloths of inexpensive paper or polyethylene. If you have two or three of them, you can cover all the shrubbery along one side of your house without the nuisance of having to shift one cover continually.

You will need scrapers. Those with double edges give you twice as much duty before dullness takes over. (Some have four edges.) Those with a single edge allow you to apply full pres-

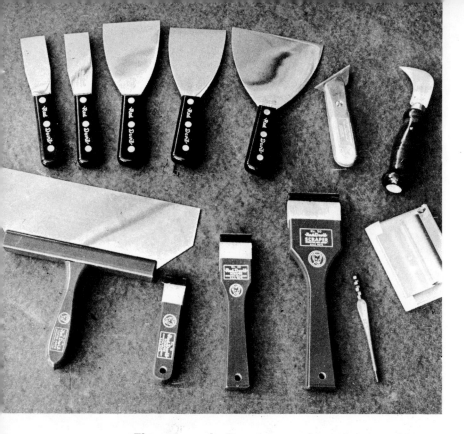

There are no duplicates among these scrapers and knives. Blades may look alike, but one is stiff, the other flexible.

sure on the scraper end without having to contend with a cutting edge.

Putty knives, besides coming in various widths, also come with stiff or flexible blades. A flexible blade is often better for scraping. A stiff blade is better for such things as pressing filler into holes.

SPRAYING EQUIPMENT. It is easier to become expert with a spray gun than with a brush. A good sprayer enables you to apply a machine-perfect finish not possible by brush, and in half the time.

Spray painting is fast, but light-duty equipment won't do a big job. A paint tank that holds one gallon is preferable to a spray cup that holds only one pint. A quart size is a good compromise for average use. For a big job, you can rent a spray rig.

Paint sprayers are heavy, and in use have to be moved continually. A mobile unit permits you to roll the equipment with ease.

Small sprayers are for light duty. Don't expect them to handle standard heavy paints or to do a house-painting job.

This 2-in-1 painting outfit can be used either for spray or roller painting. Paint supply is kept in gallon can in which paint is purchased. Control button on roller handle regulates the flow.

The smallest sprayers are self-contained and use a vibrator rather than air to eject the paint. They are all right for small hobby work, but for average home use you need the compressor-and-gun type of sprayer. Compressors may be light, inexpensive diaphragm types, or piston models which work at higher pressures and can handle heavier paint.

Judge the capability of a spray outfit by the number of cubic feet it will deliver a minute (cfm), its pressure in pounds per square inch (psi), and the size of its spray pattern. A light-duty sprayer may deliver .4 cfm at a pressure of 20 psi, with a 3″ to 4″ pattern. A medium-duty sprayer may deliver 1.2 cfm at 20 psi, with a 5″ pattern. A heavy-duty sprayer may deliver 2.7 cfm at 35 psi, with a 6″ pattern. This is by no means the limit. You can get really large equipment that may have up to a 14″ pattern and deliver 7 or more cfm.

If you have a ⅓ or ¼ hp motor, you can get a compressor separately and save. Just bolt your motor to it. It will deliver about 2.1 cfm at 30 psi.

Instead of a gun, a sprayer may use a special roller. Paint is supplied to the roller by hose so there is no need to dip it in a pan. A fingertip control in the handle regulates the flow to the roller.

SHOP PAINTING.   Although many kinds of painting and finishing are done right in the shop, it's better, because of the dust problem, to use a separate room, or at least keep the work away from where most dust is generated. Good lighting, especially natural daylight, is an advantage. Good ventilation is always essential. You may want to provide a spray booth.

The whole point of a spray booth is to confine the paint mist and keep it from spreading. Attach large sheets of paper to lightweight wood frames and hinge the frames like shutters on each side of a window. Panels may also be cut from ⅛″ tempered hardboard. Use polyethylene film to protect any part of the window that is exposed. A panel roof for the booth can simply rest on top of the two extended side panels.

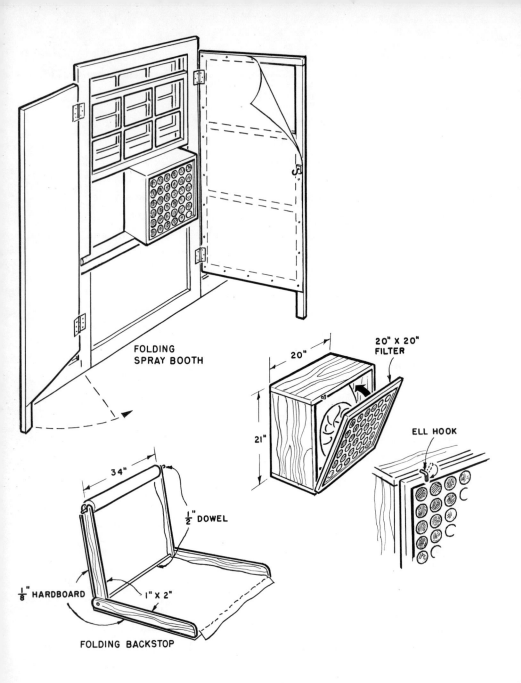

FOLDING SPRAY BOOTH

20"

20" X 20" FILTER

21"

ELL HOOK

34"

$\frac{1}{2}$" DOWEL

$\frac{1}{8}$" HARDBOARD

1" X 2"

FOLDING BACKSTOP

Spray booth for large jobs (upper left) consists of light-weight wood frames covered with paper and hinged to the sides of a window. The ventilator is a fan enclosed in a wood box equipped with a furnace filter to catch paint particles. For small jobs, a folding backstop (lower left) can be built to hold a roll of newsprint on a dowel.

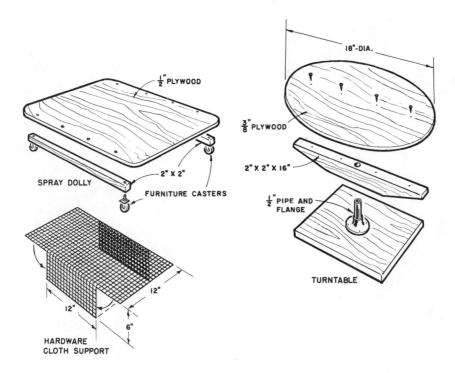

Three types of platforms for use in spray painting: a dolly
on casters for large pieces; a turntable, for smaller items,
which revolves the work and allows you to remain stationary; and a hardware cloth support for effectively covering
all sides of small objects.

Ventilation is essential. Just having the window open may
not be enough. A simple ventilator can be made by enclosing an
8″ or 12″ fan in a wood box. A 1″ furnace filter on its face will
catch paint particles and prevent their discharge outside. Be
sure the ventilating fan has a shaded-pole motor. One with
sparking brushes can ignite paint vapors.

A revolving dolly or turntable allows you to rotate work
so that you don't have to shift your own position as you spray.
If you don't have a booth, you can make a simple backstop to
catch overspray of a piece of fiberboard with newspaper thumb-
tacked to it.

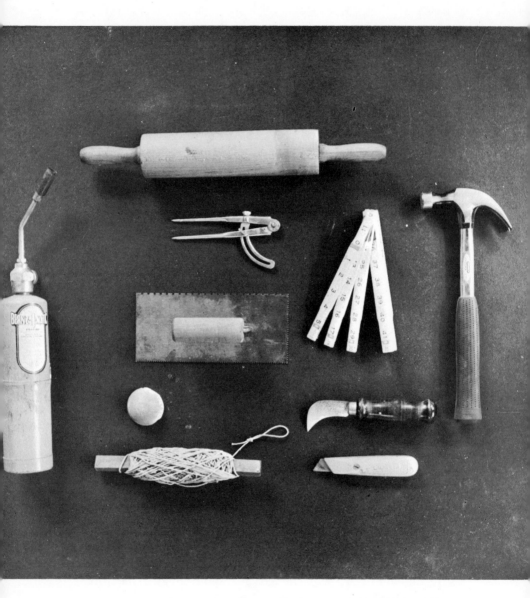

Typical kit for laying resilient flooring includes vinyl knives for cutting tile, rolling pin for flattening tile, scribers for fitting tile in irregular places, notched trowel for spreading adhestive, and a hammer, ruler, and chalk line. The torch is for softening vinyl asbestos tile as an aid in cutting.

PAPERHANGING, OTHER JOBS.   You can buy or rent complete kits for paperhanging which usually include a 6″ paste brush, a smoothing brush, a seam roller, and a razor knife. In addition, you will need a 6′ straightedge (just a straight board), a stepladder, and a working table approximately 2′ by 6′. It can be a panel of plywood mounted on sawhorses or on a pair of card tables. If you are doing much paperhanging, a wheel cutter and a wheel trimmer are helpful. You'll need a yardstick, and you may have to improvise a scaffold. A 2′-by-8′ plank between a pair of stepladders may do. For removing wallpaper, rent a steamer.

For laying resilient flooring, you'll need a pair of heavy shears for ducting today's lighter-gauge vinyl and vinyl-asbestos tiles. Solid-vinyl sheet materials are extremely tough and hard to cut, so you'll need a sharp vinyl knife. You'll need a notched trowel for spreading adhesive, or you can use a brush and brush-on adhesive. The latter is often better for it insures that you don't use too much or too little cement. For flattening down tiles, you can use an ordinary kitchen roller, but you'll be better off renting a heavy professional roller from the store where you buy your materials. A pair of scribing dividers is a useful tool. Other than that, there are no special tools—just the usual chalk line, level, square, and ruler or tape.

For installing ceramic tile, you will need a spreader, as recommended on the adhesive can. For 4″ wall tile, you will need a tile-cutting machine. It scores and breaks tiles up to ⅞″ thick with ease. You can buy a small one for about $10, or borrow one where you buy your tile. For cutting ceramic mosaic tile, get a pair of nippers—good ones. You will note that the jaws of tile nippers don't bite together.

For dry-wall or plasterboard taping you need a 5″ or 6″ knife with a flexible blade. For finishing, get a knife with an 11″ blade. Also useful is a "corner-taping tool." It makes inside corner taping fast and easy.

Glass cutting belongs in the paint department. Don't be afraid of it. It's simple—if you follow a few basic rules. One

9

Electricity / Electronics Center

Count the number of electric appliances, motors, and electronic devices in your house and you'll see why electricity and electronics commands a special department in your shop. In addition to troubleshooting and repairing equipment, you may also be extending house wiring, adding new devices, putting together electronic kits ranging from garage-door openers to hi-fi sets.

There is a saying that any electrical repair you can't make with ordinary hand tools, you can't make at all. Don't believe it. With a convenient place to work, properly arranged and properly equipped, you'll breeze through procedures you otherwise wouldn't even attempt.

THE WORKBENCH. A bench for electrical work is not the same as a woodworking bench. For one thing, it's lower. Because you'll be sitting down at this bench, make it 28″ high. Leave the underside open so you can get your legs under, as if it were a desk. An old wooden desk, incidentally, makes an excellent bench. The drawers can store all kinds of supplies and equipment. The pullout leafs provide extra working space. And a desk swivel chair is good seating.

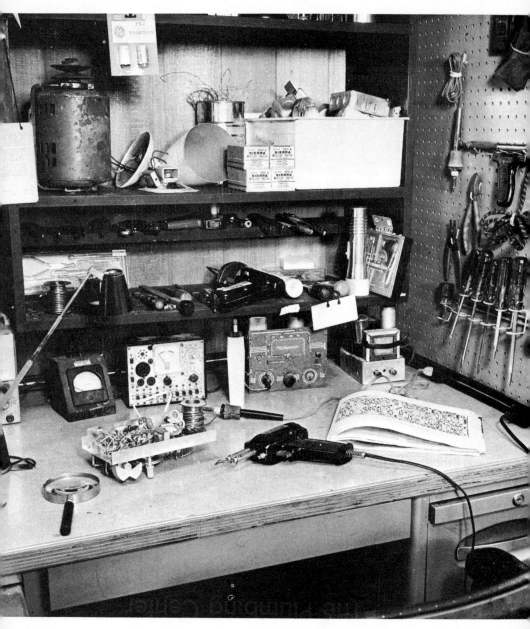

Old desk was transformed into a bench for electrical work
by applying light-colored, heat-resistant linoleum to the
top. The pullout leaves offer extra work surfaces, and
drawers provide ample storage for small parts. Electrostrip outlets run along the wall near the bench top, and a
perforated hardboard panel and shelves take care of tools
and equipment.

Any light-colored material that's reasonably heat-resistant makes a good surface for an electricity/electronics bench. Small parts are easier to see on a light-colored surface, and light reflects better. Linoleum is a good choice; so is tough, light-colored particle board.

For convenience, you'll want a variety of tools, meters, and other test equipment within easy reach. Locate the bench in a corner, or create a cubby, with wall storage on one or both sides, and you'll find it easy to surround yourself with everything you need. Shelves will give you space to put everything without cluttering up the bench top. Provide a place for hanging wiring diagrams directly in front of you.

LIGHT AND POWER.   You need better than average lighting and electrical facilities in this shop center. Where 70 FC (footcandles) is good enough general lighting for many workshop operations, electronics requires 200 FC. In addition to a 4′ two-tube reflector fluorescent lamp hanging directly above the work surface, you'll also want a supplementary lamp that you can focus directly on the work at hand.

Some photo light meters will give you a direct reading in footcandles. If you have one with ASA readings, set its film speed dial to 100 and take your reading. If you have the required 70 FC general lighting, the EV (exposure value) scale

Weston light meter (left) gives direct reading of light level in footcandles. Electronic meter (right) was assembled from a kit.

on the meter will read between 10.5 and 11. Take another reading under your supplementary lamp. If this lamp builds the light up to 200 FC, the reading on the EV scale will be between 12.5 and 13.

You should have a least a half-dozen duplex outlets or equivalent within easy reach so you can keep testing equipment and regularly used electrical tools always plugged in. Make it a 20 amp circuit. The best setup is an Electrostrip running around the sides and back of the bench just above the bench top. You can locate outlets in it anywhere you choose, change locations when you want to.

In addition, you will want a fused "test" outlet. By separately fusing the test outlet (you can use a fused plug), you'll spare yourself the nuisance of finding yourself in the dark if you short a line. Further, it should be wired through an "isolation transformer" rated at 150 watts. In servicing electrical equipment, especially AC-DC devices, you expose yourself to more than average shock hazard. An isolation transformer eliminates direct physical connection between the outlet and the power source. It can literally be a lifesaver. Typically, it comes with a 6' cord, plug, and standard AC receptacle.

ELECTRICIAN'S TOOLS.   You'll want a variety of *screwdrivers* with electrician's, cabinet and Phillips blades. The electrician's and cabinet blades have tips the same size as the shaft so they can turn screws that are deeply recessed. You'll want an 0, 1, and 2 Phillips-head driver. You'll also want at least one offset screwdriver, and one or more fine-blade jeweler's screwdrivers.

Include at least one *screw-holding screwdriver*. There are many occasions when you can't hold a screw in place by hand when you're starting to drive it. Also, it lets you hold onto the screw when it's being removed so that it doesn't drop into the works.

To turn and crimp wires around terminals, to reach into tight situations to hold wires or retrieve fallen parts, you'll

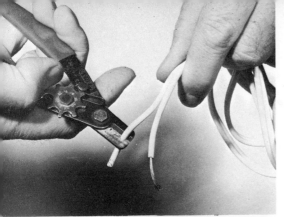

Wirestrippers adjust for removing insulation from various sizes of wire. The jaws will cut wire, too, but are not recommended for such use as they may become misaligned.

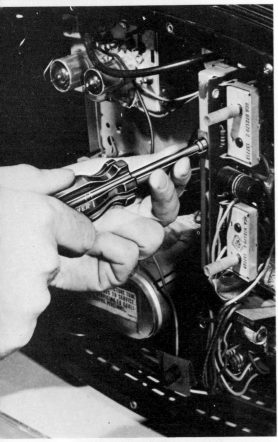

Nutdriver is a useful tool for electrical work. Some drivers fit a ratchet handle (below) for fast work.

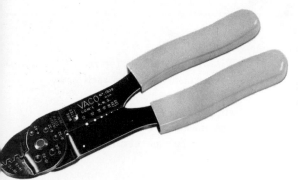

This tool cuts and strips wire and crimps solderless terminals to wire. It also cuts five sizes of bolts.

want a pair of standard *longnose pliers* and a *miniature pair*. Incidentally, there are also *pick-up tools* you can get to retrieve dropped objects. Press a plunger and the tool's jaws open; let go, and the jaws close. A pair of 10″ tweezers are also good reach-extenders.

For cutting wires to length, you'll want a pair of *oblique, side,* or *diagonal-cutting pliers*. The 5″ needlepoint are best for electronic projects. Also useful are needlenose end cutters. They'll get in and make cuts where nothing else can reach. They're especially good when you're taking old equipment apart for salvage.

You'll need a *wire stripper*. You can get an inexpensive pair that adjusts to various wire sizes so that you cut through the insulation without nicking the wire. In addition, you'll find a two-bladed *electrician's knife* useful. One blade is a combination screwdriver-wire-stripper. The other is a spear blade.

Nut drivers are useful. You can get one that adjusts to any size hex nut. If you get separate drivers, a ³⁄₁₆″, ¼″, ⁵⁄₁₆″, and ⅜″ will take care of most chassis work. Get ones with handles that are color-coded for quick size identification. Though sometimes awkward to use, a *dog-bone wrench* is a useful alternative. It will fit ten hex-nut sizes, but it often requires more swing room than is available.

SOLDERING EQUIPMENT. Consider getting both a soldering iron *and* a soldering gun. The iron has a resistance wire heating element coupled to a soldering tip. It takes a minute or two to heat up, because the tip is heated by conduction. In a typical soldering gun the heating element *is* the tip. When you pull the trigger, it heats up in three or four seconds.

The advantage of a gun is that it heats up fast. One advantage of an iron is that it holds its heat. This means you can use it to solder a joint on an electrical line after turning off the circuit. Another advantage is that you can get a pencil-type soldering iron that weighs only ounces. It won't ruin delicate jobs, such as soldering a phono cartridge. But it won't solder a heavy connection. For that you need a heavier iron or a gun.

The job of a soldering iron or gun is not to melt the solder but to heat the metal to be soldered. Solder isn't an adhesive. It performs a chemical action, dissolving metals from the material being joined and forming an alloy. The amount of heat a soldering tool delivers is usually determined by its wattage. For small and heat-sensitive work, a 40-watt tip is insurance against damage.

You can get guns with interchangeable tips, so you can match tip to work. The heavy tip may use 100 to 200 watts. The medium, 50 to 100, and the light 25 to 100. A power rating indicates the size of the joint a tool is capable of soldering, but it doesn't necessarily indicate its working temperature. Most of the jobs you'll want to do can be handled by a low-power iron.

Instead of a single-loop tip, some guns have a single-post design. It has an indirectly heated tip and uses a copper heating element. A single-post gun drawing 100 watts is said to deliver twice as much heat as the conventional iron. But it takes about twelve seconds to heat up—three or four times longer than the single loop.

Soldering tools can do more than soldering. There are special tips for cutting plastic, removing old putty, and for burning identification on wood handles. A smoothing tip can be used for welding plastic. It's also good for sealing freezer bags and taking dents out of furniture. In the latter case, put a damp

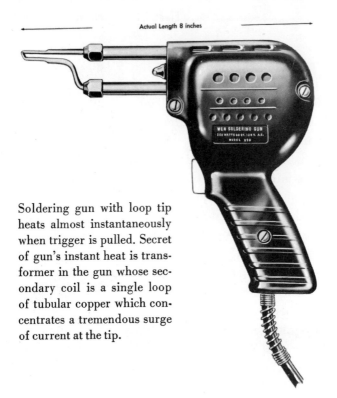

Soldering gun with loop tip heats almost instantaneously when trigger is pulled. Secret of gun's instant heat is transformer in the gun whose secondary coil is a single loop of tubular copper which concentrates a tremendous surge of current at the tip.

rag over the dent, then touch it with the tip. The steam will make the wood fibers swell and the dent will disappear. The smoothing tip will also melt stick wax or shellac to seal scratches and nicks.

Solder is the alloy that holds the connection together. A mixture of tin and lead, when molten it has the capacity to dissolve (not melt) copper. The best solder for electronic wiring is about 60 percent tin and 40 percent lead. Joints to be soldered must be clean. Flux helps with this cleaning by dissolving surface oxides and it is often incorporated in wire solder as a core. Acid flux leaves corrosive residues that will ruin the operation of electronic equipment. For this reason rosin flux is recommended for electrical and electronic work. It doesn't present this problem.

You'll need a heat sink for soldering transistors, diodes, and other components that are readily damaged by heat. But

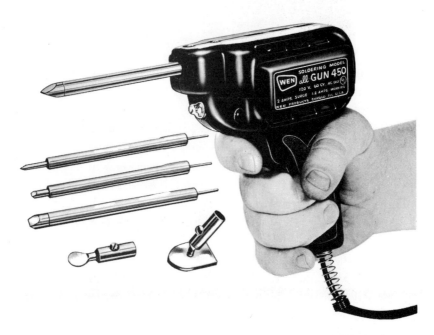

Single-post soldering gun is lighter than most single-loop guns, has readily changeable tips. Special insulation and a temperature-control switch enables it to use a copper heating element from which heat is conducted to the tip.

This is not a soldering gun but a pistol-grip soldering iron. It has no transformer; conduction from a resistance element heats the tip.

you probably don't have to buy one. One is likely to be included in any kit you assemble.

TEST EQUIPMENT.   One of the most useful tools for troubleshooting is a *continuity checker*. Wires burn out, break, or become disconnected. A continuity checker will enable you to tell if this has happened. It can tell you if a switch or fuse is good. It can tell you if the windings in a motor armature are intact. *Testing is always done on disconnected equipment, never on live circuits.*

One of the simplest continuity checkers is a "clicktester." It's easy to make. It consists of an earpiece, like that used on a transistor radio, a C or D flashlight battery (even an old run-down one), and some wire. Solder a 4″ piece of insulated wire to the top center connection of the battery as a probe. As a second probe, solder another similar length to one terminal of a jack that will accommodate the tiny plug of the earpiece. Run a short wire from the other jack terminal to the bottom of the battery and solder. For convenience, tape the jack to the battery. That's all there is to it.

Simple clicktester is made from a D cell and an earpiece. Current has to travel through suspected part to make a click. If there is no click the circuit is open.

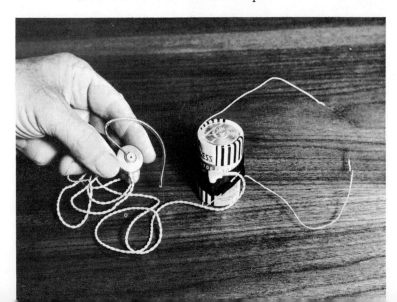

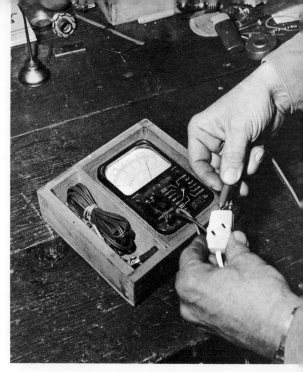

VOM meter enclosed in a box to protect it against damage. It is being used to test the output of an extension cord.

To test the condition of a switch, touch the two probes to the switch terminal screws. With the switch on, you should hear a click in the earpiece. With the switch off, there should be no click. You can test electric bulbs, fuses, motor windings, etc.

The clicktester has limitations. It can't distinguish between the extremely low resistance of a short circuit and the relatively low resistance of some normal circuits. For such accurate evaluation, you need an instrument such as a volt-ohm-meter (VOM). You can assemble one of these instruments yourself from an inexpensive kit. A VOM measures both volts and ohms, AC as well as DC.

In testing appliances and other equipment for malfunctions, you check the resistance in ohms against what the normal resistance should be. A variation indicates a malfunction. It's very valuable, for example, in checking the value of a resistor. You can tell immediately if it's gone bad. An electric clock, for another example, usually measures between 700 and 1000 ohms. Touch the probes to the prongs of the clock cord and you immediately know if the clock and motor winding are good. If the meter shows no reading, you know that either the cord or motor is open.

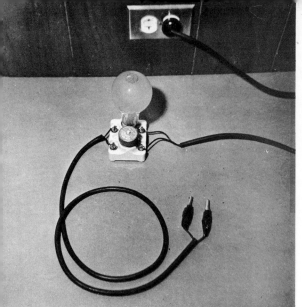

Test light works on the same principle as a clicktester, but requires more careful handling because of line voltage. Circuit breaker is handy for resetting in case of a short.

A socket and bulb, as shown here, can be used as a test light to determine when an outlet or circuit is live.

Neon test quickly indicates if the current is reaching motor terminals. Lack of light indicates trouble is in the cord or supply, not the motor.

Hand-size, digital VOM features five functions, 22 ranges with a single selector switch. It's battery or AC operated.

Self powered Handy Dandy, by Burnworth, uses two penlight batteries, tests appliances, car headlights, fuses, anything electrical with electricity off.

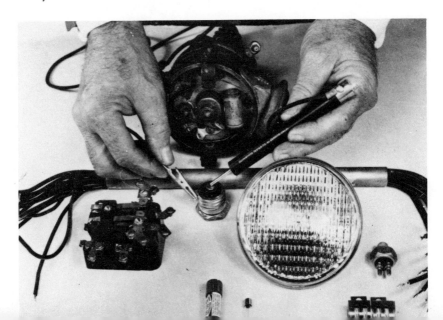

A test lamp is another simple but invaluable aid in troubleshooting. You can make your own of a lamp and socket fitted with two test prods, or you can buy an inexpensive neon tester. You'll use it to determine when electricity is reaching a wall outlet, terminals, or any specified point along a line or circuit.

There is other equipment you may find useful in electric and electronic work. You can get transistor checkers, electric fence and low-voltage testers, and battery testers.

There is a receptacle tension tester to assure that there is a firm and constant electrical and mechanical contact with the blades of an attachment plug.

There is a receptacle circuit tester that indicates whether the receptacle is correctly wired, or if it has reverse polarity, an open ground, neutral or hot wires, hot or ground wires reversed, or if the hot is on neutral and the neutral is unwired.

For use with this circuit tester, there is a receptacle tester that can determine if the receptacle is protected by a properly operating GFI (ground fault interrupter)..The device has a neon lamp. If the lamp goes out, the GFI is operating properly. If it stays lit, the GFI is not functioning and the receptacle could be a source of dangerous shocks.

10

The Plumbing Center

When you consider all the plumbing jobs that have to be done around the house, you can appreciate the importance of a plumbing center in your workshop. In some instances you can handle a simple job with general-purpose tools, but most often you'll find the work easier and the results better if you have tools designed specifically for plumbing. Read the following descriptions of typical plumbing problems and the tools needed to cure them; then decide what you need for your plumbing center.

CLOGGED DRAINS. This usually tops the list of plumbing complaints, and the No. 1 tool for the job is the *force cup*. It does just what its name implies: it forces clogging material free so that it can be washed down the drain. You can get force cups (also called plungers and plumber's helpers) designed for sinks or toilets. If you get a two-way variety, you can use it for either. For toilet use it has a flange that folds out.

The second important tool for opening clogged drains is the *auger*, the tool to use when a force cup fails. A closet auger is used for clogged toilets. It is short—usually 5½"—and has a protective rubber guard. For clearing other drains and traps

This plumbing center occupies 4' of wall space. Tools are hung on perforated hardboard panel. Plastic trays and juice cans hold assorted fittings and small parts.

Three-inch force cup is a handy tool for clearing clogged drains. Folded washcloth is used to seal off overflow drain. Petroleum jelly applied to the rim of the cup gives it a better grip (right).

Closet auger is used on clogged toilets when force cup fails. Power auger fits chuck of an electric drill and handles tough cleaning jobs.

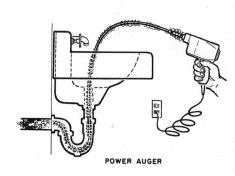

POWER AUGER

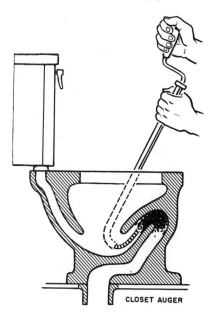

CLOSET AUGER

there are hook-end or corkscrew-tipped augers ranging from 15′ to 50′ in length. Some are "self-storing." These are a great convenience, and the container into which the snake coil fits prolongs its life and makes it easier to use. For average use, the 15′ auger is the one to buy. If the rare occasion arises when you need a longer one, you can always rent it. There are flat "sewer rods," which come in lengths up to 100′ with blades ¾″ wide. Some augers are of thin clockspring steel. Others, of coiled spring steel, are flexible in every direction.

Power augers are available which fit ¼″ or ⅜″ electric drills. These electric snakes, 6′ and 12′ long, are designed for home use. They work best in drills with variable speeds and a forward-reverse switch.

Opening or removing sink traps is one of the most commonplace solutions for clogging. It is sometimes necessary to remove the trap to insert an auger. Any smooth-jawed wrench can do an acceptable job of removing the nuts without marring

Slip-and-lock wrench and hex wrenches are best tools for getting a nonslip grip on multisided nuts and fittings.

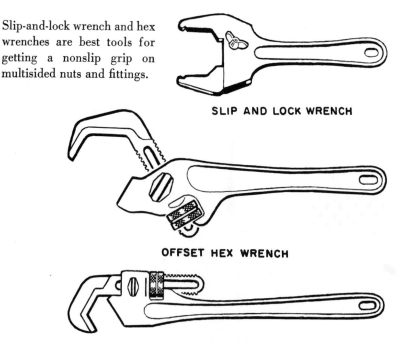

SLIP AND LOCK WRENCH

OFFSET HEX WRENCH

HEX WRENCH

chrome-plating, but an adjustable *slip-and-lock nut wrench* is made specially for the purpose. So is a *hex wrench*, without question the best tool for getting a nonslip grip on multisided nuts and fittings. Its jaws are smooth, so they won't mar plated finishes, and they are narrow, so they fit in close quarters. A hex wrench looks like a pipe wrench, except that its jaws have an elbow crook to fit the hex shape. It comes in sizes with nut capacities up to 3 inches, but the size that handles 1½″ sink and tub drain nuts is all you're ever likely to need. Besides the standard straight hex wrench, you can also get offset designs especially made for working in tight places.

WATER SUPPLY PROBLEMS.   Faucets are the biggest troublemakers. They drip, chatter, or leak at the spindle. Replacing washers calls only for a smooth-jawed wrench and a screwdriver, but if washers wear out faster than they should, and it takes extra-heavy twisting to completely shut off the

Pump pliers with smooth jaws also handle hex nuts when a trap must be removed during a drain-cleaning operation. Bucket to catch water is a necessity.

Replacing a worn washer in a faucet is only half the job if the seat onto which it fits is rough or pitted. A faucet seat dresser can frequently restore seats so they work properly.

Basin wrench is needed to remove inaccessible nuts when installing a new faucet.

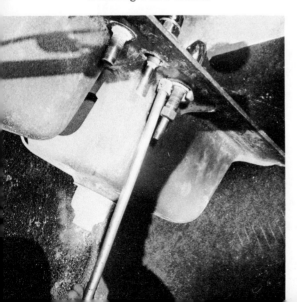

BASIN WRENCH

flow, there may be trouble in the faucet seat. That requires a *faucet seat dresser* or *reamer*. It will smooth the unevenness that is the cause of the trouble.

These drip-stoppers come in seven sizes. Standard faucets have a ⅝″ bevel, utility faucets ¾″, and small faucets ⁹⁄₁₆″ or ½″. Get a kit with three cutters and you'll be able to handle almost any faucet.

When a seat is in hopeless condition, you can use a *new-seating tool* to tap threads in the seat and then screw in a new seat with a screwdriver.

Sometimes an ailing faucet can be saved by replacing its spindle or its entire inner workings. At other times, commonsense dictates replacing the entire faucet, especially if it's an obsolete variety. To remove a faucet and install a new one means getting up behind the basin, and the only way to do it is with a *basin wrench*. You'll find this tool useful in getting at other inaccessible nuts. It belongs in every well-equipped plumbing center.

Internal pipe wrench is used for removing broken pipe, closed nipples, or other fittings when it's impossible to get an external grip. Turning the mandrel forces gripping dogs against inside of fitting; then it is turned with a wrench or, in some models (photo), with a handle that is integral with the tool.

INTERNAL PIPE WRENCH

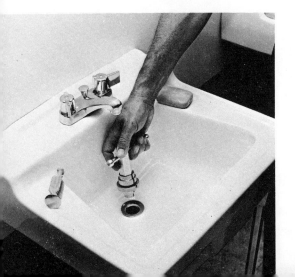

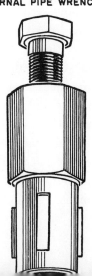

Lack of water pressure may be caused by a well pump whose pressure switch is set too low, by supply pipes that are too small, or by pipes whose capacity has been reduced by scale-like deposits of minerals. These deposits are usually most severe in hot water lines. They may also create an insulating lining in the water tank so that it is impossible to get enough hot water. Scale clogging also makes pipes whistle, bang, and shudder. The easiest way to solve the entire problem is to install a water softener. The softened water will gradually reabsorb the deposits and restore pipes and water heater to near original condition. The tools needed for this job are enumerated in the section that follows.

INSTALLING NEW PLUMBING.   Your project may be as simple as installing an outside hosecock, or as ambitious as putting in an entirely new bathroom. In either case, you will have to work with pipe. You will have to work with pipe if you install a new fixture to replace an old one, install a dishwasher, a clotheswasher, a water softener, a new water heater, a swimming pool, an underground sprinkler system, all or part of a heating system, or new pipes to supplant those that have burst or deteriorated. The tools you need depend on whether it is galvanized steel pipe, or copper or brass tubing.

Copper tubing is the easiest to work, and requires the fewest and least expensive tools. In many cases, you can use copper tubing even though the rest of the plumbing is something else. The transition from steel to copper is made with adapters.

Copper tubing may be cut with a *hacksaw* or a *tubing cutter*. Choose the tubing cutter. It is less work, and it unfailingly produces a square cut. If a cut isn't square, tubing won't recess all the way into fitting sockets and leaks will result. You can get an inexpensive tubing cutter that will handle up to 1″ or 1½″ outside diameter tubing, and a considerably more expensive cutter that will handle 1″ to 3⅛″ outside diameter tubing. You need this large cutter only if you are working on drain and vent pipes.

Tubing cutter always produces a square cut. This one contains a reamer for removing burrs which can cause leaks or clogging.

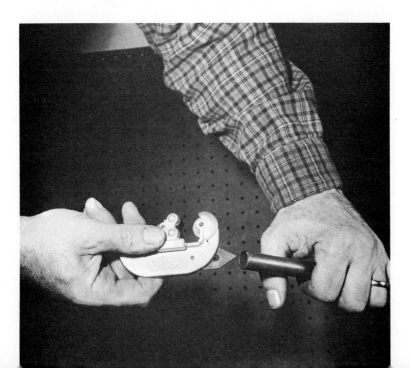

There will be some situations in which you can't use a cutter. That's when you need the hacksaw. The blade is most important. Select one with twenty-four teeth to the inch.

Tubing is either rigid or flexible. Rigid tubing makes a neater installation. You'll use flexible tubing only when you have to snake pipe into existing walls or it is desirable to reduce the number of fittings. For short-radius bending of tubing with ¼″ to ⅝″ outside diameter, get a set of *spring steel bending tubes*. They help prevent kinking tubing. Alternately, you can fill the section to be bent with damp sand. Clean thoroughly afterwards.

Copper tubing is usually assembled by "sweating" or soldering. For soldering either rigid or flexible copper tubing, get a 1 pound spool of 50/50 solid wire solder (half tin, half lead) and either a 2-ounce or a 1-pound can of soldering paste.

Tubing sockets and pipe ends must be thoroughly clean before soldering. For cleaning the tubing ends get a "plumber roll" of *emery cloth*. The cloth is only 1½″ wide and you tear off a strip 4″ or 5″ long for use. If you don't use it all for plumbing, you'll find it has a myriad other applications. For the fittings, get a *copper-fitting brush* for ½″ or ¾″, whichever you are using. You can also get outside copper-fitting brushes in the same sizes. Less satisfactory for cleaning tubing and fittings, but usable, is steel wool.

A standard *propane torch* does an acceptable job in soldering. The only job for which it is undersized is 3″ copper drainage systems. It takes too long to heat up the joints. If you're doing a complete bathroom installation, you may wish to rent a professional plumber's torch or get a gasoline torch. The latter requires unleaded gas and is a nuisance to start, but it does have a big, hot flame.

When joints in copper tubing are ones that may have to be disassembled (like an oil-burner filter, for example), flare joints may be used. Typical *flaring tools* for copper, aluminum, brass, and thin-wall tubing can handle sizes from ⅛″ to 1″. Kits are available that include a flaring tool, a bender set, and

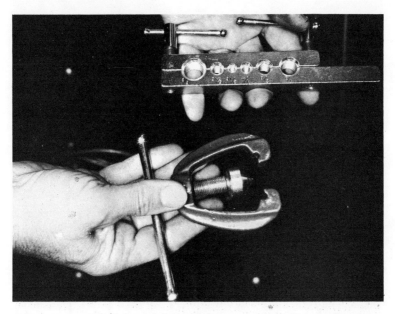

Flaring tool for making connections in copper tubing.

a tubing cutter—all compactly housed in a metal storage box.

Tools for working with steel and iron pipe are considerably more expensive than those for working with copper. You'll need a *pipe vise* or a *machinist's vise* that has pipe jaws. You'll need a *pipe cutter,* a *pipe threader set,* and a *burring reamer.* You can get most of what you need in a kit. If you have only a limited amount of work to do, you can buy pipe in various lengths already threaded. Short lengths of pipe already threaded are known as nipples, and having a few of these on hand never does any harm.

Other supplies you'll need are *pipe-joint compound* and a small stiff brush for spreading it, *plumber's wicking* for wrapping around joints, and *plumber's putty* for setting strainers, faucets, sink rims, etc.

Cast-iron pipe generally requires lead joints. Lead is applied on top of oakum—5 pounds of lead for a 4″ pipe. To pack oakum and lead into joints requires *calking irons,* which come in a variety of shapes to match different situations. At one time only molten lead was used for such joints and a special

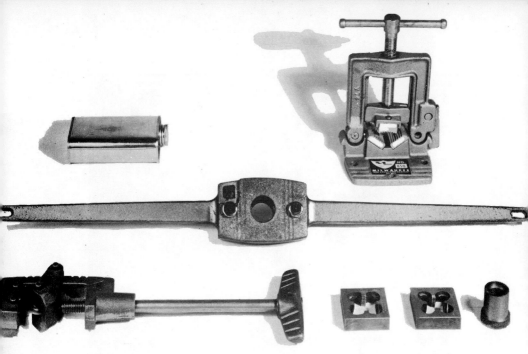

Complete kit for cutting and threading steel pipe.

Dies for threading steel pipe come in several sizes, all fit the same handle.

Steel pipe is held in special vise (right) which works by latch action. Cutter requires considerable room to revolve around pipe (below), but vise is detachable and need not monopolize bench space.

asbestos joint runner was needed to contain the lead. Also involved were a cast-iron melting pot and some means of heating the lead, usually a gasoline furnace. Alternately, cold shredded lead, or lead wool, might be used instead of molten metal. Now, codes permitting, there is a lead seal that can be applied over oakum and no heating is required. A pint seals four 4″ joints. Cast-iron pipe is cut with a hammer and cold chisel, sometimes with a hacksaw and hammer.

Flexible plastic pipe is used for pumps, sprinkler systems, and swimming pools. Rigid plastic pipe has similar uses. It is standard pipe for built-in central vacuum systems. Such pipe may be cut with a hacksaw or tubing cutter, though a special wheel for plastic tubing is available. Joining is made with solvent.

For doing major plumbing installations, a ½″ *electric drill* and at least three large self-feed bits are almost a necessity. These bits are expensive, but in time and work saved and the workmanship produced, they are a good investment. A ⅞″ power auger will provide passageway for ½″ pipe, a 1⅛″ for ¾″ pipe. A 2⅛″ will accommodate 1″ and 1½″ pipe. A 2⁹⁄₁₆″ is for 2″ pipe.

The plumber's favorite tool for notching studs and joists and cutting through floors is a *reciprocating saw*. A *saber saw* is best for making counter cutouts for installing sinks. To do the cutting necessary in running some pipes, a *keyhole saw*, a *ripping chisel*, and a *star drill* or *masonry bits* may be needed.

11

Concrete / Masonry Center

What are the jobs around the house requiring concrete, brick, flagstone, and mortar?

There are repair jobs—cracks in sidewalks, broken steps, chimneys that lean, walls that need new mortar, stains of all kinds, basements that leak.

There are building jobs—a new patio, paving around a pool, a barbecue, fireplace, steps, garden wall, a foundation for a new addition, a block garage.

There are enough of both kinds of jobs to require a sizable collection of tools and supplies, and a special place to keep them. Your own collection will depend on the jobs you tackle. Let's consider repairs first.

STAINS. Efflorescence, soot, grease, mortar—these are only a few of the stains that make concrete and masonry unsightly. To remove them you'll need rubber gloves, an eye shield, a stiff-fibered scrub brush, and a variety of stain-removing agents. Muriatic acid is the classic masonry cleaner. If you get mortar stains on brick, flagstone, or tile, it does a great job of removing them. But there are many other equally good, sometimes better cleaners that you'll find at your masonry or build-

Here is one homeowner's concrete/masonry center with tools and supplies for handling building jobs. The 20-gallon refuse can contains sand.

Stiff-fibered scrub brush and a masonry cleaner are often all that's needed to remove efflorescence stains caused by moisture bringing salts to the surface and depositing them during evaporation.

ing dealer. Many cleaners are formulated especially for removing oil and grease stains from garage floors and driveways. Trisodium phosphate is the prime ingredient in many of them.

To prevent stains, there are clear, transparent silicone sealers which are applied with a paintbrush. They help keep water from penetrating masonry, and stains from sticking. They are recommended for preserving the cleanliness of grout in tile walls, particularly in showers. Clear sealers can control concrete "dusting." Sealers for brick, flagstone, and marble are important in your arsenal. You'll be collecting various kinds, and for convenience you'll want to stock them all in one place—your concrete/masonry center.

CRACKS, HOLES, CRUMBLING MORTAR.   The first step in almost any concrete or masonry repair is to chisel out cracks and pick away all loose material. A *hammer* and a ⅜″-cut or ½″-cut *cold chisel,* a *bricklayer's hammer,* a 2- or 3-pound *mash* or *drilling hammer,* a *pointed chisel,* and a *small fiber brush* or *whisk broom* will all be useful. You'll need a

Chisel end of a brick hammer (left) is a good tool for removing loose concrete when making repairs. Cold chisel (right) is also an aid in repairing cracks in concrete.

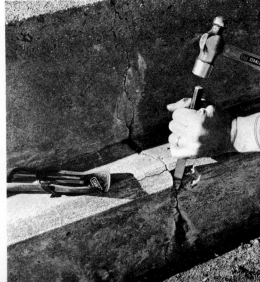

sledge for breaking up old paving, a *railroad pick* for lifting and resetting sections of walk that have settled or buckled.

For digging mortar out of brick joints, a handy tool is a *tuck pointer's rake*. As an aid in holding and feeding new mortar into a joint, you can improvise a *hawk,* which is nothing more than an 8″-by-8″ square of board with a dowel or other handle attached to its underside. You can also use a *steel finishing trowel* as a hawk.

For compacting mortar in joints, you'll need a *jointer* like those used for new bricklaying work. It can have V-shaped or rounded ends to make the style of joint required. If joints are to be filled flat and flush, get a *caulking trowel.* These are available with blade widths from ¼″ to 1″ to match joint requirements. If joints in either brick or stone are to be deeply recessed, you can improvise a *raker* from a scrap of wood with a nailhead projecting as far as the desired jointing depth.

You can mix your own patching material, but you'll find better ones already prepared. Latex patchers are especially good because they can be feather-edged. Epoxy patchers are expensive, but none is more durable. You can buy prepackaged

Homemade hawk (left) is used when jointing brickwork to hold and catch mortar. Steel finishing trowel can also serve as a hawk (right).

If you mix your own patching material, it's a good idea to include a bonding agent and an antishrink agent.

If joints in brick or stone are to be deeply recessed, improvise a raker from a scrap of wood and a nail that projects the depth of the joint.

mixes in bags that contain cement, sand, lime, and other additives. You merely add water. For extensive work you'll find it cheaper to mix your own. Store sand, cement, and lime in refuse cans or other containers that will protect them against moisture. Moisture will quickly cause sand to break through a paper bag.

LEVELING TOOLS. Whatever your building project, you will need one or more levels to keep construction plumb, hori-

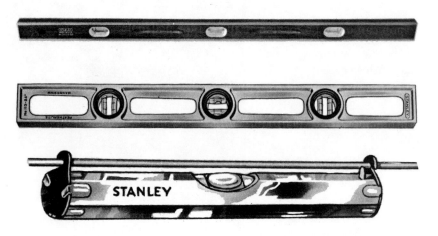

Three useful levels for concrete/masonry work (from top):
48″ wood mason's level; 2′ aluminum level; and line level.

zontal, or at any desired pitch. The mason's favorite is a 4′
brass-bound *mahogany level*. The 4′ length is a good one because it provides a more accurate reading over long spans.
The wood is recommended because it is comfortable to touch in
any weather.

Walls, walks, and other construction are kept in alignment
by means of *lines*. Cotton line is cheapest. Nylon outlasts it
many times, but is costs more than twice as much. You can get
cotton or nylon lines in green, white, or yellow.

The best way to insure that lines are perfectly horizontal
is by means of a lightweight line level which hooks right on the
line. *Corner blocks, lineholders,* and *line pins* are devices to
which line ends are fastened. For block, an *aluminum stretcher*
is a favorite. You can easily make your own line holder out of
a 4″ scrap of 2-by-4 cut into an L-shaped piece.

When exacting accuracy is essential, such as for a foundation wall, a *transit* insures that it will be dead level. Rent or
borrow one. For less demanding work, you can get a sighting
device that thumb-screws to a level.

A 50′ *steel tape* is almost a necessity when building walks,

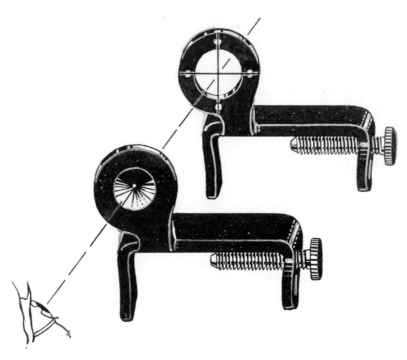

This sighting device attaches to the ends of a level and offers a quick means of getting a reading over a fairly long distance. For more demanding work, use a transit.

Aluminum line holder (left) adjusts to the width of concrete blocks. Homemade holder (right) is simply an L-shaped block with a hole in the corner and a groove along the top to hold the line.

walls, and patios. Just attempt to do it with a 6' folding ruler.

For a firm, level base for slabs and paving, you can use a *garden roller*. You'll also need a *tamper*. You can buy one, or you can quickly knock one together. Make its head of heavy stock, nail a 5' handle to it, and you're ready for business.

CONCRETE WORK.   A *cement boat* or *mortar box* is a necessity for mixing any sizable amount of mortar. Make the sides out of 2-by-8s tapered at each end, the bottom and ends of tongue-and-groove boards. Make it at least 2' wide and 5' long and you'll have plenty of space in which to operate. It may leak a little when you start, but the cement will soon plug it up. You will need a *mortar hoe*. A garden hoe won't do. It's too small. A mortar hoe has a 10" blade with two holes that expedite the mixing process.

For mixing and holding small batches of mortar, you can use a *mortarboard*. It is simply a platform 30" by 30" of tongue-and-groove boards nailed to a pair of 2-by-4 runners.

For building forms to hold concrete, you'll need the

To get a firm, level base for slabs and paving you need a garden roller (left) and a tamper (right). The latter can be homemade of heavy wood.

Rent a power-driven mixer if you have a moderate amount of concrete to prepare. For over a yard, it's advisable to have it delivered.

Two important tools for finishing concrete are shown here: a wood float, in worker's left hand, for rough finishing; and a steel trowel for smooth finishing.

Groover is a special tool for creating patterns or joints on an unsightly plain slab of concrete. Run it back and forth along a straight board.

Power trowel does a fast job in hot weather when concrete may set too quickly if troweled by hand.

following tools: *saw, hammer, level, rafter square, 50' tape, rule, line, hacksaw, pliers* and a *wrecking bar* for disassembly.

You can mix concrete on the sidewalk or driveway or on the basement or garage floor, but be prepared to do a good hosing down afterwards to prevent staining.

The hardest thing about concrete and masonry work is the mixing. Rent a small *electric-* or *gasoline-powered mixer* and you'll cut the work to a fraction.

If you have a yard or more of concrete to mix, you'll be much better off having it delivered. Be prepared with *barrows, shovels,* and *rakes* to spread it as required. The usual home wheelbarrow holds only 3 to 3½ cubic feet. A contractor's wheelbarrow holds 4½ to 5 cubic feet, but before you get one remember that each cubic foot of concrete weighs about 150 pounds.

Troweling is a lot of work too. For a rough finish, you'll use a *wood float.* For a smooth finish, you'll use a *steel trowel.* Rent a *power trowel* and you'll again save yourself a lot of work.

TOOLS FOR BRICKLAYING. For laying mortar when building with brick, you'll need a *brick trowel.* This tool comes in blade sizes from 8½″ to 12″ long. A 10½″ blade is a popular choice.

You'll also need a *pointing trowel* with a blade 5½″ to 6″ long. It's handy for all kinds of small jobs.

Three indispensable tools for bricklaying (top to bottom): set for cutting brick; brick hammer for chipping brick; trowel for applying mortar.

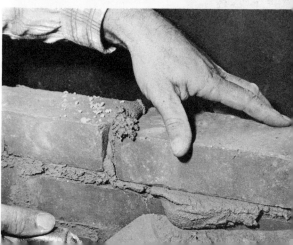

Mirrored image of mason's ruler shows standard inch markings on one side. Other side has ten different brick-spacing scales.

Brick hammers range in weight from 10 to 32 ounces. Most men are comfortable with one weighing between 20 and 26 ounces.

For cutting brick, you'll want a *bricklayer's set* or *chisel*. These come with blades 2½″ to 4″ wide. The 4″ bit is most popular.

The *mash* or *drilling hammer* is used with star drills for cutting holes. Hammers come in 2-, 3-, and 4-pound weights. Get one that's right for your own size and strength. Masonry bits for your electric drill cut down on the effort of drilling holes.

You may want a special *brick-mason's rule*. It will help you calculate where courses fall.

12

The Metal Shop

You don't need a machine shop to work with metal. This is fortunate, for every home handyman has to work with sheet, angle, and tubular metals. He has to work with heating, ventilating, and air-conditioning ducts, appliances, gutters, and leaders, vehicles, metal furniture. He needs the basic tools for drilling, cutting, and joining metal.

You may want more than the bare essentials. You may want to set aside a corner of your shop for working with metal and include a welder and a metal lathe. If you have a drill press and a grinder in your woodworking shop, these should be located near the metal center. They are as important in metalworking as in woodworking.

The simple bench shown in the drawing is designed for welding, brazing, and casting. The top of the casting area of the bench is covered with asbestos and is 6″ lower. The brick-top area, used for brazing, can also accommodate a small smelting furnace. The welding area of the bench is copper-topped. To complete the metal shop, there might also be a bending brake and metal roll, and a power hacksaw.

METALWORKING LATHE. This is the toolmaker's tool, and the heart of any full-fledged metal shop. It is the tool for

COPPER
TOP

BRICK TOP

WELDER   BIN FOR RODS   BRAZING
TANKS

CASTING BENCH

SAND BIN

Bench for a metal shop has three kinds of surfaces: copper for welding; brick for braising; and asbestos for pouring metal into molds. Space beneath the bench is divided into compartments for storing equipment.

gunsmiths, auto mechanics, modelmakers, and inventors. Besides turning metal, it can drill, mill and cut threads. It's a precision tool, and thus one of the most expensive.

In operation and appearance it resembles a wood lathe. Both have a fixed headstock and a movable tailstock. But there the resemblance ends. The metal lathe is designed to endure the most rugged demands and work to the closest tolerances. It has a massive, precisely controlled carriage. The carriage offers provision for feeding the work along the tool bed, squarely across the bed, or at a compound angle to it.

On a metalworking lathe, spindle revolution may be geared to carriage travel, making precision thread-cutting possible. By varying the gears, you can vary the ratio of carriage travel to spindle speed. Cross speed may be automatically controlled.

Lathe size is determined by the diameter of the largest piece of work the machine will turn. This is called its "swing." Typical swings are 6″, 9″, 10″, and 12″.

Popular for home use is the midget lathe that will swing diameters up to $2^{15}\!/_{64}$″. Called the Unimat, it will also function as a miller, borer, drill press, and grinder.

THE DRILL PRESS.   In a machine shop, a drill press ranks second to a lathe. In a home-oriented shop, a drill press comes out on top in usefulness because it works wood as well as metal and is handy for grinding, wire brushing, even shaping.

Drilling metal usually requires greater precision and control than drilling wood. That's why you need a drill-press vise for holding work. Some adjust to holding work at any angle from 0 to 90 degrees.

A portable electric drill can do some of the same jobs as a drill press, but it lacks precision and control. You can improve these qualities by providing a drill stand for it.

CUTTING AND BENDING METAL.   A hacksaw, snips, and chisels are the standard assortment of hand tools for cutting metal. Among power tools, a table saw, radial saw, saber saw and band saw are all adaptable to the purpose.

To cut soft aluminum, copper, and brass with a table or radial saw, you need a small-toothed, taper-ground, nonferrous blade—or a carbide-tipped slotted blade with eight or twelve teeth. Steel-cutting "cut-off wheels" should never be used on a bench or radial saw. Whenever you cut metal, always wear protective goggles.

You can cut light metal with a saber saw fitted with a 32-tooth tungsten blade. Reciprocal-type power hacksaws cut at 90- to 45-degree angles, but this is not a tool for the average home shop.

With special blades, band saws adjustable to slow speeds can be used for cutting metal. You can buy slow-speed convertors for reducing blade speed on some band saws at a 10:1 ratio.

A brake is the professional's tool for bending metal. For the homeowner, a machinist's vise often suffices. You can extend its jaws with a pair of angle irons. Soft metals, like aluminum, can be bent in a straight line with a simple jig. The jig is no more than a saw kerf in a length of wood. The edge to be bent is inserted in the kerf.

A steel pounding block will spare your bench top from a lot of abuse when there is metal to be hammered into shape. The ball-peen hammer is most used in metal work. One with a 12-ounce head is about right for average duty, but you can get heads from 4 to 32 ounces. Polished metal surfaces are damaged by steel hammers so for some operations you will want a plastic-tipped hammer, a rubber-tipped mallet or equivalent.

JOINING AND FINISHING.   Simplest joining is often by means of sheet-metal screws or rivets. Galvanized metal, copper, and aluminum can be soldered. You may use solder to join copper flashing, gutters, copper liners and planters. Solder and a torch are the classic way for joining or repairing joints in galvanized rainware.

There is a special solder and flux for stainless steel. For copper, nickel alloys, and soldering aluminum to dissimilar metals, there is an aluminum brazing alloy and flux.

You can buy inexpensive welders to do your joining jobs, but they are adequate for only the lightest duty. Electric welders require special power supplies. The minimum for even the smallest welder is a 30 ampere line. Most welders require 40 to 60 ampere circuits.

Among other tools needed in finishing are files for dressing metal to size, removing burrs, fins, and ragged edges. A small portable electric sander-polisher is also useful. With an aluminum-oxide disc, it can perform many metal grinding and finishing operations. It is good for grinding down welded joints.

Arc welders let you weld, cut and pierce metal, also braze and bend. There are models for almost any pocketbook. Welder shown is one of many models offered by Wards.

13 | The Craft Shop

Carpentry, masonry, plumbing, electrical work—they are essential in running a house, but they don't tell the whole shop story. A vast array of other activities may command your interest and require shop facilities. These interests may include pottery, photography (still or movie), modelmaking, weaving, wood carving, upholstery. If you bind books, carve soap, tie flies, make guns, or work with silver, leather, or plastics, you will want a place to pursue these hobbies.

In many cases, a special bench, and storage facilities for its special tools and equipment will handle a hobby interest within the shop. Shop tools can then be shared, as required, with the hobby. That can be a great convenience and asset.

In most cases, handicrafts and hobbies do not involve the use of noisy machinery, nor do they produce large volumes of debris. That means they can be separated from the main shop and be included within living areas without running into problems. Spare bedrooms, attics, and other space not ideal for woodworking shops can beautifully accommodate handicrafts. These places usually have better natural light. Many hobbies integrate nicely into playrooms or family rooms. When a hobby is the special interest of a younger family member, the shop can often be located in the child's bedroom.

This shop, devoted exclusively to crafts and hobbies, includes work areas and equipment for ceramics, painting, modelmaking, and moviemaking.

Corner of craft shop (right) contains modelmaking bench equipped with a jigsaw, vise, and a 12"-high drill press. The saw can be adapted for sanding, grinding, and buffing. Behind is a movie-editing center with splicing equipment.

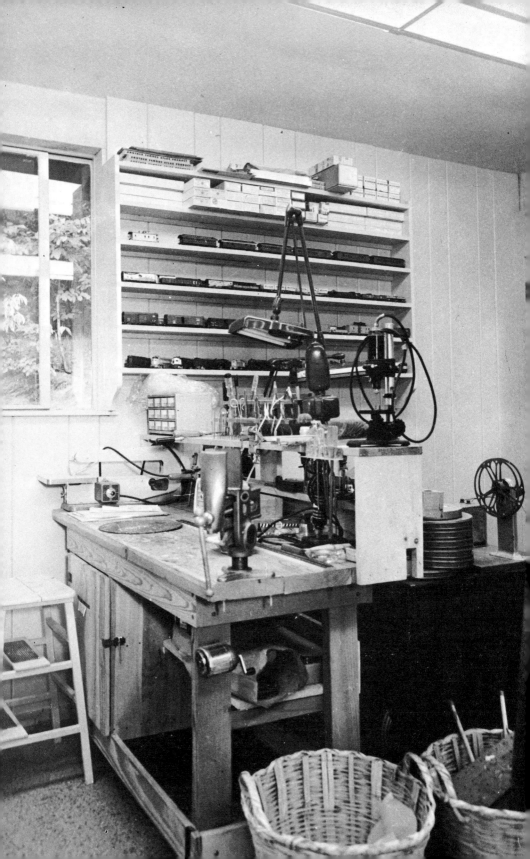

Design is often the key to success in many crafts. In this shop a corner is set aside for a desk and drawing board lit by an overhead fluorescent fixture.

A HOBBY CABINET.   Often half the work of pursuing a hobby is getting materials out and putting them away. A good cabinet can enclose everything needed for many hobbies. When not in use, with its top shut, a cabinet can present a good appearance regardless of how disreputable things may look inside.

The cabinet shown, designed by A.M. Warcaske for Rockwell Manufacturing Company, incorporates some of the best ideas found in industrial benches and results from years of experience in varied handicrafts. It has such a variety of facilities that it is adaptable to practically any type of hobby. Closed, the bench lid is a stand-up work surface for such jobs as cutting leather, upholstery, cloth, stencils. With the top set at an angle, it becomes a drafting board, with an instrument drawer conveniently located at its right. At the bottom of each drawer section is a file for catalogs, plans, instructions, letters.

With the top folded back, the sit-down work surface is ready for business. It faces the folded-back top, which is a good place to tack wiring diagrams or other plans or instructions. The work surface itself is hardboard and has a cutout with mortises for bench pins of various sizes. Just below the cutout is a trash drawer. You can do wood carvings right at the edge of the cutout and have most of the waste fall directly into the drawer.

The trash drawer is lined with sheet metal so it can be easily cleaned. A vise can be mounted right over it. Insert a bench pin in one of the mortises and you have a handy surface for working on small parts.

Below the trash drawer is a "jeweler's apron." It's a shallow drawer with a canvas bottom and is a lifesaver when working with small parts. Whatever you drop gets caught by the apron, and doesn't fall on the floor and roll out of sight.

Most of the hobby bench is made of ¾" plywood. Fir may be the least expensive, but if the bench will be located in a living area you may want to use a cabinet-grade hardwood plywood. It will give the cabinet a real "furniture" look. Assemble all parts of the bench with glue and finishing nails. Set

This craft bench has storage space and work surfaces to accommodate a variety of hobbies—modelmaking, handicrafts, electronics. Chair has high and low seats for different working conditions.

Swinging out hinged end-pieces lets the top slope forward to become a drafting board. Bottom drawer is size to hold file folders. Shallow drawer is designed to hold drawing instruments.

Space between the two work surfaces of the bench permits leaving out work in process. Storage at the back is for long items like lumber and tubing.

Plans for Building the Craft Bench.

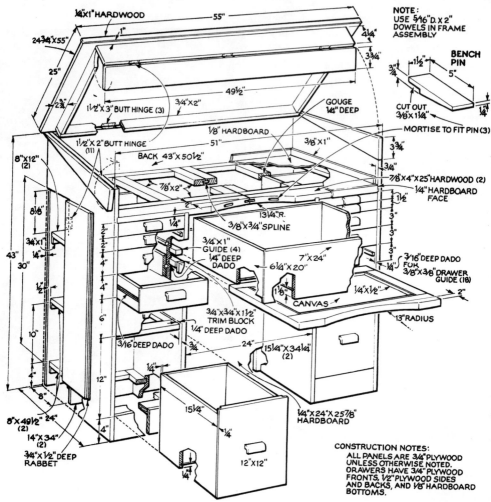

the nails just below the surface and fill the holes with wood dough or putty.

Shown with the bench is a high-low stool. It is designed for either bench level. Make it of a fine hardwood, like walnut, equip it with a velvet pad, and it will be a piece worthy of any man's castle.

Here is an orderly procedure for building the bench:

1. Make the drawers and the two drawer compartments.

2. Dado end panels and glue drawer slides in place.

3. Build the frame for the bench top in two sections and join them with a hardwood spline.

4. Screw the hardboard surface to the top, so it can be replaced when worn.

5. Use a ⅜″ mortising bit to cut holes for bench pins.

6. Attach shelf cleats for back compartment.

7. Use screws to attach bench top, back panel, and knee-hole panel. The bench can then be easily disassembled for moving.

DARKROOM.   Photo processing ranks high among hobbies. If your shop is in a basement, you may have enough space to wall off one corner of it for a darkroom. But photo work has little relationship to shop activities, so it's just as well to put the darkroom elsewhere if it's more convenient.

You can set a darkroom up in a bathroom or a closet, but if you can find an area about 6′ by 10′ elsewhere, take it. A 5′-by-5′ space is generally regarded as the mininum for a complete one-man facility. A spare room in a living area of the house is good, but it must not be too large. A sprawling darkroom is inefficient, wasting motion and energy.

At first consideration in establishing a darkroom is the availability of running water, preferably both hot and cold. A basement is usually more desirable than an attic merely because water is more likely to be available. If you're in a basement and the location is below sewer level, you can probably provide a pump, codes permitting, to take care of drainage. In a basement, put down a duckboard floor so you won't have the discomfort of standing on concrete for long periods.

You'll need working surface and storage. The working

If darkroom is located below sewer level, a pump arrangement like this one can handle disposal of waste water.

surface should be large enough to accommodate your enlarger and three trays. The best height for the working surface depends on how tall you are and which height you find most comfortable. It will probably range somewhere between 30″ and 36″. You'll need storage for paper, film, and chemicals. Keep the paper and film away from hot-water pipes and heating ducts. Heat and humidity spoil them.

Next comes the problem of darkness. It's easier to make a room dark than to bring water to it. If there is a window, you can buy a lighttight shade or a blackout blind, or equip it with a fitted sheet of plywood. To stop light leaks, entrance doors may require weatherstripping.

Lightproof darkroom fan, made especially for photographic use, exhausts stale air into basement area.

The room should be lighttight, but the walls do not necessarily have to be painted flat black. In fact, it is preferable to enamel the walls a light color so they reflect a maximum amount of safelight.

As for arrangment of facilities, if you are right-handed, you'll find that your work will progress most conveniently from right to left, and the reverse if you are left-handed.

For ventilation, you'll need one or two lightproof fans designed for photographic use. If you have two fans, use one to bring in fresh air, the other to exhaust stale air. That will make a positive continuous flow. You can get by with only one fan that exhausts air if you provide a lightproof intake.

POTTERY.   This is a craft that can be carried on in a garage or basement, or in a spare room in a living area. It can share space with other creative activities such as painting and weaving.

Pottery requires running water, or easy access to it. There may be need for a high-amperage circuit if you have an electric kiln, or gas supply if yours is fired by that fuel.

Potters wheel and kiln are basic equipment for the craft of pottery. Special heavy-duty cable has been run to service electric kiln, which needs a high-amperage circuit.

The principle item of equipment, beside the kiln, is a wheel, either kick- or power-driven. It is unlikely that you will acquire either a kiln or a wheel without previous experience in working with clay, so by the time you are ready for them you'll know what you want. Storage is needed for clay, glazes, completed work, and work in process.

Working with clay is messier than some other crafts. The floor should be durable and easily maintained. Concrete or resilient sheet material are satisfactory.

THE INFORMATION CENTER.   Everyone who engages in a craft knows how many books, magazines, and articles he collects on the subject. Keeping them all in one place is a big help in tracking down a particular bit of data or a design idea. The unit shown makes organizing such material easier.

Every craft shop needs an information center. This wall-hung chest can accommodate books, clippings, catalogs, and plans.

Plans for Building the Information Center

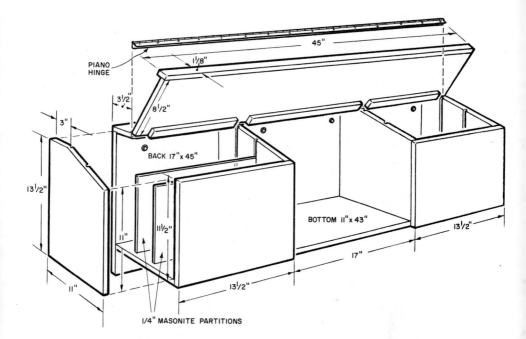

With its lid down, it's a stand-up desk that hangs on the wall and occupies no floor space. A convenient shelf holds books, magazines, catalogs.

Lift the lid, and you find two file compartments that can hold clippings, instruction sheets, correspondence, and other data.

All parts of the information center can be cut from a 4'-by-6' panel of ½" plywood. Masonite partitions slip into slots cut halfway back in the file compartments to keep material vertical when the files are only partially filled. Butt joints fastened with screws and glue are used throughout.

14

The Portable Shop

Many maintenance jobs have to be done on location. This means carrying tools, nails, other supplies and equipment to where you are working. In some cases, it means transporting them in a car. You'll find it highly convenient to provide easy portability.

HOLSTERS. The simplest kind of carriers are strong leather tool holders that attach to your belt. A simple loop with two belt slots will accommodate a hammer. You'll find it espe-

Leather holsters enable you to carry small tools on your person when working on jobs outside the shop.

cially useful when climbing a ladder. Another type of single-tool holder is a pocket about 4″ wide and 6″ high, into which you can slip a pair of pliers, a folding ruler, etc.

Other holders may have from three to five pockets of various sizes. In addition, some may have one or more side loops and a T chain to hold a roll of electrician's tape. Some are fitted with harness snaps for holding small tools.

Everyone is familiar with canvas carpenter's aprons, often given away as promotional items by lumberyards. You can buy strong, tough carpenter's aprons made of heavyweight leather. Instead of just one or two nail pockets, they may have four, and in addition a variety of tool pockets, slots, and loops. Instead of tying them around the waist with a string, you have an adjustable web belt which quickly hooks together.

SIMPLE TOTEBOXES.   Carriers for supplies can be made of scrap wood, plywood, and hardboard. You can design these carriers to fit in a drawer or hang on a wall. Attach a strap to a carrier instead of a handle and you can sling it from a shoulder for occasions when you need both hands free.

You can put compartments in a totebox so that tools and supplies fit individually. A saw, a hammer, a torch, chisels—each can have a special place.

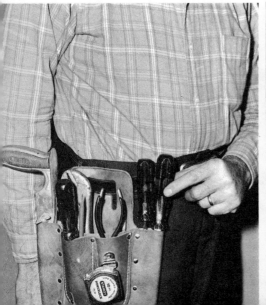

Here are two good tricks:

Slot an extra leg on one side of your totebox so it can be tightened by a wing nut in any position. Then you can set the box level on any roof regardless of its pitch.

Bothered by the wood chips and sawdust that collect in your totebox tray? Make its bottom of hardware cloth and the debris will sift through instead of piling on your tools.

There are portable tool caddies you can buy. Unlike the usual toolbox in which you have to rummage to find what you want, these are organized so that tools are easily accessible.

Different kinds of nails are kept separately in this 8-compartment carrier. It is sized to fit into a workshop drawer when not traveling.

Small totebox built of scrap wood holds hammer and oil can in clips at each end, screwdrivers in holes drilled in inside brace. The tray has room for a variety of tools.

Commercial totebox has thirty-nine tool-holding slots, two storage wells for large items, and four small drawers for nails, screws, etc.

Large metal totebox has cantilever tray which swings up for access to tool-storage compartment below.

Tools can be stored in a strategic place in the house in kit which attaches to back of closet door. When minor repairs must be done, you don't have to tote tools from the shop to the job.

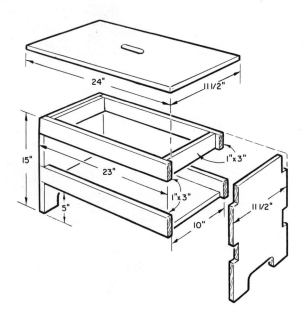

THE MINI-BENCH. For many on-location jobs, you need a sawhorse, a step stool, and a work surface. You can build a "mini-bench" which can perform all these functions.

It's really an old-fashioned carpenter's bench which you can quickly knock together out of 1"-by-12" stock. A good height is 16"; a good length, 24". Brace the bench with a shelf-tray about halfway up and you'll have a convenient place for carrying tools and supplies. Apply glue to all joints before driving screws or nailing and you'll have a miniature work-bench sturdy enough to take all the sawing, hammering, and drilling you do. The mini-bench's 16" height will let you reach an 8' ceiling. Cut an oval slot in the center of its top to accommodate your four fingers and carrying it will be no problem.

CARRY-ALL.   This open-style chest, designed by Masonite, offers the advantage of a perforated hardboard tool rack so that everything is accessible. You can build the carry-all in the size shown, or in a smaller model, with tray dimensions reduced to 12″ by 24″ and hardboard to 24″ by 24″. The cutout for a hand-hold means you'll always pick up the carrier at a point where it balances.

Carry-all holds a large number of tools in side compartments and on perforated hardboard rack. Hand-hold should be cut in the exact center so the totebox balances when picked up.

Build the basic box first, joining the ends to the sides with nails and glue. Hardboard bottom fits in saw kerfs cut in the sides. Uprights and plywood end panels are nailed and glued from the inside to the end pieces.

TRAVELING ASSISTANT. You can travel in style with a 7-in-1 assistant like that shown in the photograph. It has special holders for tools. A plane fits into a holster at one end. At the other end, two springs support a propane torch. Chisels and bits can be kept in the removable tool tray. A handsaw slides into a slot behind a small-parts bin.

Plans for Building
the Carry-All Totebox

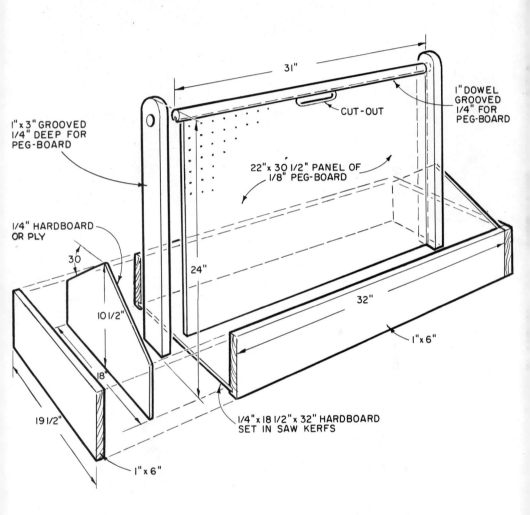

1"x 3" GROOVED
1/4" DEEP FOR
PEG-BOARD

1" DOWEL
GROOVED
1/4" FOR
PEG-BOARD

31"

CUT-OUT

22"x 30 1/2" PANEL OF
1/8" PEG-BOARD

1/4" HARDBOARD
OR PLY

30

24"

10 1/2"

32"

1"x 6"

18"

19 1/2"

1/4"x 18 1/2"x 32" HARDBOARD
SET IN SAW KERFS

1"x 6"

The top of the traveling assistant is adjustable. At its lowest position, it serves as a step stool. Raised all the way, it's at sawhorse height. Swung to one side, the top is a support for work that must be held vertically. The box includes a duplex grounded receptacle. Its cord winds up on a built-in spool when not in use.

Traveling assistant is a self-contained workshop that not
only carries tools to the job but functions as a sawhorse,
miter box, and step stool once there. Here the adjustable
top is raised to its full height and used as a sawhorse.

Swung sideways, the top acts as a clamping surface to hold
boards for planing or routing. Duplex grounded receptacle
on the extension outlet lets you plug in power tools at your
feet. Cord winds up on built-in spool.

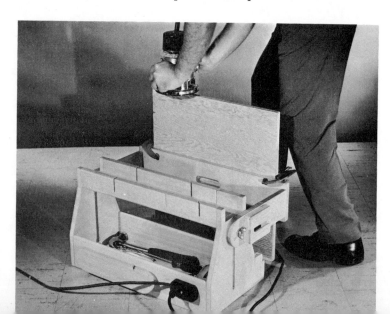

Tilting the top to form a V with the side creates a handy holder for working on tubing and other round stock.

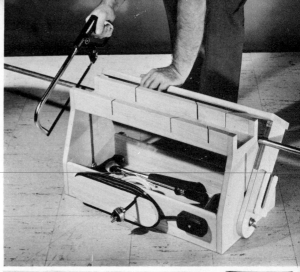

With top out of the way, the miter box is free to handle angle cuts. Box should be made of hardwood.

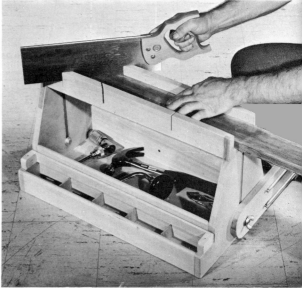

When top is adjusted to this position, the springs on one end hold a propane torch in place. Braze bolt heads and pin washers, as shown in the plans, to keep them from turning when wing nuts are tightened or loosened.

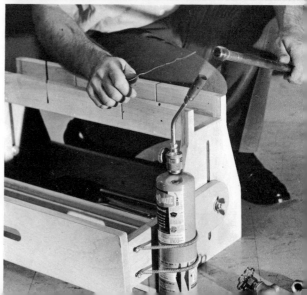

Plans for Building the Traveling Assistant

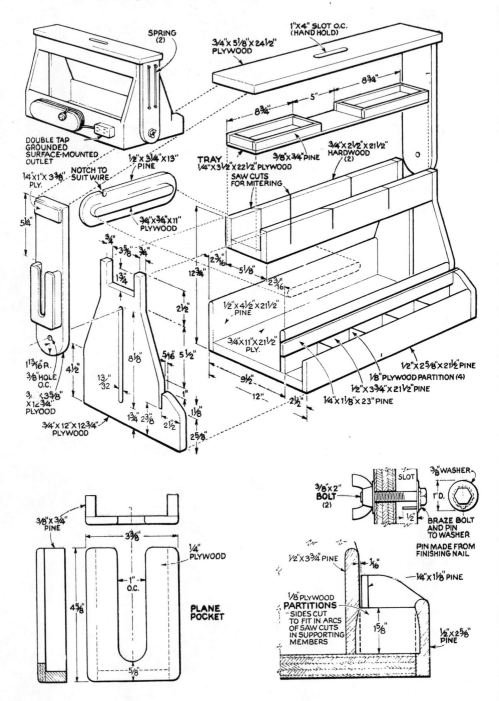

SPRING (2)

DOUBLE TAP GROUNDED SURFACE-MOUNTED OUTLET

NOTCH TO SUIT WIRE

1/4"X 1"X 3 3/8" PLY.

1/2"x 3/4"x 13" PINE

5 1/4"

1 13/16" R.
3/8" HOLE O.C.
3/4"X 3 5/8" X 12 3/4" PLYWOOD

3/4"X 12"X 12 3/4" PLYWOOD

3/4"
3 5/8" 3/4"
1 3/4"

8 1/2"

13/32" O.C.

1 3/4" 2 3/8" 2 1/2"

1 1/8"

2 5/8"

4 1/2"

5/16" 5 1/2"

2 1/2"

12 3/4"

2 3/16"

5 1/8"

2 3/16"

9 1/2"

12"

2 1/2"

1"X 4" SLOT O.C. (HAND HOLD)

3/4"x 5 1/8"x 24 1/2" PLYWOOD

8 3/4"

8 3/4" 5"

3/8"x 3/4" PINE

TRAY
1/4"X 3 1/2"X 22 1/2" PLYWOOD
SAW CUTS FOR MITERING

3/4"X 2 1/2"X 21 1/2" HARDWOOD (2)

1/2"X 4 1/2"X 21 1/2" PINE

3/4"X 11"X 21 1/2" PLY.

1/2"X 2 5/8"X 21 1/2" PINE
1/8" PLYWOOD PARTITION (4)
1/2"X 3 3/4"X 21 1/2" PINE
1/4"X 1 1/8"X 23" PINE

3/4"X 3/4"X 11" PLYWOOD

PLANE POCKET

3/8"X 3/4" PINE

1/4" PLYWOOD

3 3/8"

1" O.C.

4 5/8"

5/8"

3/8"X 2" BOLT (2)

SLOT

3/8" WASHER

1" D.

1/2"

BRAZE BOLT AND PIN TO WASHER

PIN MADE FROM FINISHING NAIL

1/2"X 3 3/4" PINE

1/16"

1/4"X 1 1/8" PINE

1/8" PLYWOOD PARTITIONS
- SIDES CUT TO FIT IN ARCS OF SAW CUTS IN SUPPORTING MEMBERS

1 5/8"

1/2"X 2 5/8" PINE

Most of the traveling assistant is built of plywood and pine. Its miter box, however, should be made of a solid hardwood lumber like maple. Assemble with nails and glue. After assembly, round all sharp edges and sand smooth. Then finish the box with several coats of shellac.

ROLLING TOTEBOX.   This portable tool box, designed by the American Plywood Association, can be carried like a suitcase. It holds a complete carpentry kit. If you wish, you can attach ¾″ wheel casters to the bottom to make handling easier.

Because of the weight of the tools it will carry, this chest should be assembled with rabbet joints, and nailed and glued. Use 4D and 6D finishing nails and a waterproof glue.

Rolling totebox has rack for two saws, drawers for small tools, and larger compartments for bulkier items. It is built entirely of ¼″, ½″, and ¾″ plywood.

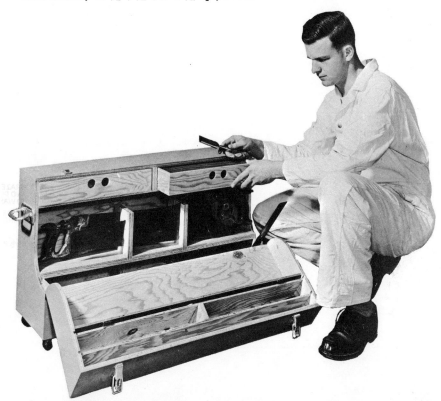

Plans for Rolling Totebox

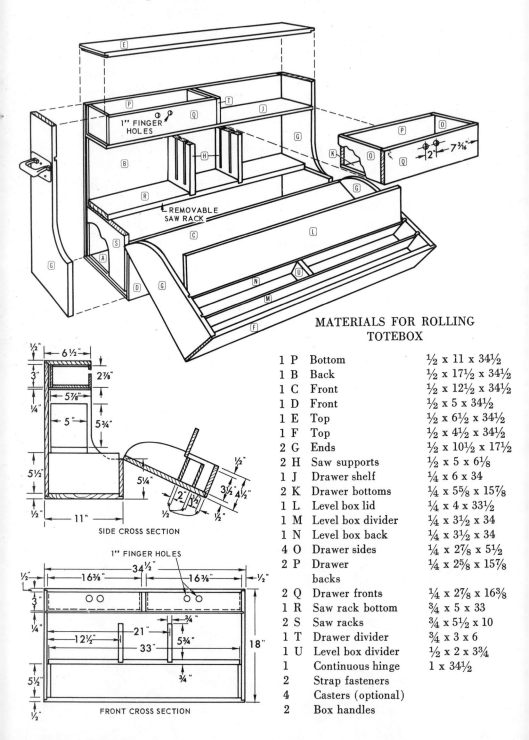

1" FINGER HOLES

← REMOVABLE SAW RACK

SIDE CROSS SECTION

1" FINGER HOLES

FRONT CROSS SECTION

MATERIALS FOR ROLLING TOTEBOX

1	P	Bottom	$\frac{1}{2}$ x 11 x 34$\frac{1}{2}$
1	B	Back	$\frac{1}{2}$ x 17$\frac{1}{2}$ x 34$\frac{1}{2}$
1	C	Front	$\frac{1}{2}$ x 12$\frac{1}{2}$ x 34$\frac{1}{2}$
1	D	Front	$\frac{1}{2}$ x 5 x 34$\frac{1}{2}$
1	E	Top	$\frac{1}{2}$ x 6$\frac{1}{2}$ x 34$\frac{1}{2}$
1	F	Top	$\frac{1}{2}$ x 4$\frac{1}{2}$ x 34$\frac{1}{2}$
2	G	Ends	$\frac{1}{2}$ x 10$\frac{1}{2}$ x 17$\frac{1}{2}$
2	H	Saw supports	$\frac{1}{2}$ x 5 x 6$\frac{1}{8}$
1	J	Drawer shelf	$\frac{1}{4}$ x 6 x 34
2	K	Drawer bottoms	$\frac{1}{4}$ x 5$\frac{5}{8}$ x 15$\frac{7}{8}$
1	L	Level box lid	$\frac{1}{4}$ x 4 x 33$\frac{1}{2}$
1	M	Level box divider	$\frac{1}{4}$ x 3$\frac{1}{2}$ x 34
1	N	Level box back	$\frac{1}{4}$ x 3$\frac{1}{2}$ x 34
4	O	Drawer sides	$\frac{1}{4}$ x 2$\frac{7}{8}$ x 5$\frac{1}{2}$
2	P	Drawer backs	$\frac{1}{4}$ x 2$\frac{5}{8}$ x 15$\frac{7}{8}$
2	Q	Drawer fronts	$\frac{1}{4}$ x 2$\frac{7}{8}$ x 16$\frac{3}{8}$
1	R	Saw rack bottom	$\frac{3}{4}$ x 5 x 33
2	S	Saw racks	$\frac{3}{4}$ x 5$\frac{1}{2}$ x 10
1	T	Drawer divider	$\frac{3}{4}$ x 3 x 6
1	U	Level box divider	$\frac{1}{2}$ x 2 x 3$\frac{3}{4}$
1		Continuous hinge	1 x 34$\frac{1}{2}$
2		Strap fasteners	
4		Casters (optional)	
2		Box handles	

3-COMPARTMENT TOOLBOX.   This big box is just the thing when an extensive tool collection must be moved on location. Its large panels are of ⅜″ exterior plywood, and its top, bottom, and sides are of 1″ lumber. Piano hinges are used for the three tool sections and a pair of 2″-by-3″ hinges for the plywood cover. Canvas straps, broom clips, wood latches, wood brackets, and metal L braces may be used to hold tools securely. The plywood cover may be lined with foam rubber to keep smaller items from rattling.

When the plywood cover is closed on its compartment, the unit can be swung shut on the middle compartment. These two compartments together match the thickness of the remaining compartment upon which they close and are latched. The toolbox may now be carried like a suitcase.

This 3-compartment toolbox was designed by the American Plywood Company after study showed that carpenters often spend more time hunting for a tool than using it. The compartments open up to display every tool in its own place, instantly visible and within easy reach.

Plans for Building
3-Compartment Toolbox

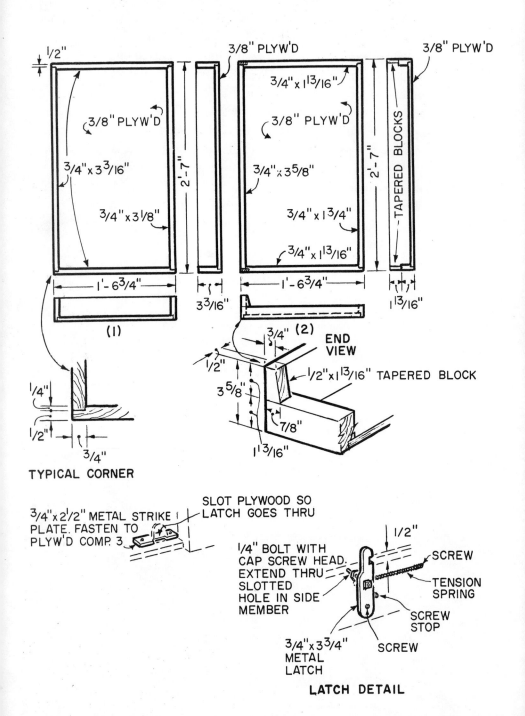

1/2"

3/8" PLYW'D

3/8" PLYW'D

3/8" PLYW'D

3/4" x 1¹³/₁₆"

3/8" PLYW'D

3/4" x 3³/₁₆"

3/4" x 3⁵/₈"

2'-7"

TAPERED BLOCKS

3/4" x 3¹/₈"

3/4" x 1³/₄"

3/4" x 1¹³/₁₆"

2'-7"

1'-6³/₄"

(1)

3³/₁₆"

1'-6³/₄"

1¹³/₁₆"

3/4" (2)

END VIEW

1/2"

1/2" x 1¹³/₁₆" TAPERED BLOCK

1/4"

3⁵/₈"

1/2"

7/8"

3/4"

1¹³/₁₆"

TYPICAL CORNER

3/4" x 2¹/₂" METAL STRIKE PLATE. FASTEN TO PLYW'D COMP. 3

SLOT PLYWOOD SO LATCH GOES THRU

1/2"

1/4" BOLT WITH CAP SCREW HEAD. EXTEND THRU SLOTTED HOLE IN SIDE MEMBER

SCREW

TENSION SPRING

SCREW STOP

3/4" x 3³/₄" METAL LATCH

SCREW

LATCH DETAIL

214

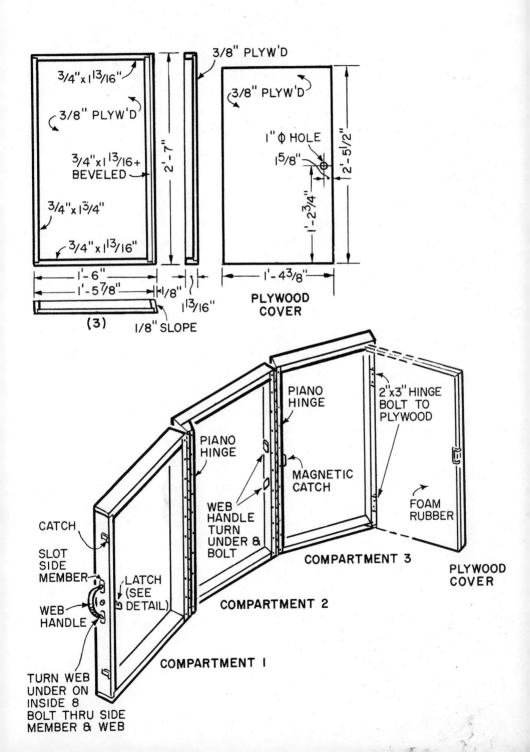

3/8" PLYW'D

3/4"x1¹³/₁₆"

3/8" PLYW'D

3/4"x1¹³/₁₆+
BEVELED

3/4"x1³/₄"

3/4"x1¹³/₁₆"

2'-7"

1'-6"

1'-5⁷/₈"

1/8"

1¹³/₁₆"

(3)   1/8" SLOPE

3/8" PLYW'D

1" φ HOLE

1⁵/₈"

2'-5½"

1'-2³/₄"

1'-4³/₈"

PLYWOOD
COVER

PIANO
HINGE

PIANO
HINGE

2"x3" HINGE
BOLT TO
PLYWOOD

PIANO
HINGE

MAGNETIC
CATCH

WEB
HANDLE
TURN
UNDER &
BOLT

FOAM
RUBBER

CATCH

SLOT
SIDE
MEMBER

LATCH
(SEE
DETAIL)

WEB
HANDLE

COMPARTMENT 3

PLYWOOD
COVER

COMPARTMENT 2

COMPARTMENT 1

TURN WEB
UNDER ON
INSIDE &
BOLT THRU SIDE
MEMBER & WEB

With each compartment approximately 31" high and averaging over 18" wide, it can hold enough tools to build a house. It was designed by the American Plywood Association, who call it the Tamap tool box. The letters of the word Tamap stand for time and motion American Plywood. The design was originated because a study revealed that carpenters often spent more time hunting for a tool than in actually working with it. This toolbox was organized so that every item is clearly visible and easy to reach.

CASTERS are the important aid to mobility. Using two swivel and two fixed casters is best for most shop purposes. Having fixed casters at front, swivel at rear, makes it easier to follow a straight line. For increased maneuverability, put swivels at front and the fixed ones at the rear. But don't use four swivel casters unless maneuverability is more important than straight-line travel. They are uncontrollable if you have to push for any distance.

For heavy-duty use, you may wish to use six casters. In this case, use four swivels—one at each corner—and two fixed casters in the middle.

For moving table or radial saws, a hand truck or wheelbarrow arrangement works well. For this setup, place fixed casters or wheels at rear of stand only, no wheels at front. To move the saw, lift its front end so the rear wheels are free to roll. Use four casters if you want to make your saw stand into a swinger. It will turn in a tight circle. But make sure the two front casters are equipped with locking levers or brakes. For most situations, 2½" plate-type casters do the job.

Index